D1348952

ARCHITECTURE 11

ARCHITECTURE 11

RIBA BUILDINGS OF THE YEAR

TONY CHAPMAN

RIBA ₪ Trust

MERRELL
LONDON · NEW YORK

First published 2011 by

Merrell Publishers Limited
81 Southwark Street
London SE1 0HX

merrellpublishers.com

British Library Cataloguing-in-Publication Data:
Architecture 11 : RIBA buildings of the year.
1. Architecture – Awards – Great Britain – Periodicals.
2. Architecture – Awards – Europe – Periodicals.
I. Chapman, Tony, 1950– II. Royal Institute of British Architects.
720.7′941′05-dc22

ISBN 978-1-8589-4561-3

Produced by Merrell Publishers Limited
Picture research by Clemency Christopherson
Designed by Alexandre Coco
Indexed by Vicki Robinson

Printed and bound in Slovenia

A SNAPSHOT OF
THE PROFESSION
TONY CHAPMAN, HON FRIBA

Architectural awards are sometimes called a snapshot of the state of the profession. If that's the case, these days the image being presented is more negative than positive, such is the profession's current state. It's not the fault of the architects, it's not even the fault of the awards, it's the economy, stupid – and our politicians' stumbling attempts to deal with it.

The last politician to attempt to build a way out of recession (I'm not counting the postwar period, that's different) was Franklin D. Roosevelt in 1930s America. And it worked. With his New Deal – a move that would have had him indicted as a Red in the McCarthyite 1950s or the Tea Partite 2010s – FDR dared to preach and practise the doctrine that it was better to invest in people than in markets, in infrastructure not unemployment. New Labour was good at spending easy money, Lottery funds that were neither strictly its own nor entirely ours – grey money or free money, depending on your point of view. It espoused the Tories' Private Finance Initiative on the same grounds: in the fantasy world inhabited by accountants, funds thus provided did not count as public expenditure, so it should be OK with the *Daily Mail* and therefore the voters would vouchsafe the party another term. In the end we voters saw through Labour's stratagems and instead gave our blessing to a shotgun marriage – sorry, coalition government – wherein the Lib Dems were allowed a place at the top table so long as they promised to keep quiet. Now localism rules; it sounds cuddly – surely, this is the stuff of government by the people for the people *etc.*, *etc.* – but it's not. It's a fig leaf for cuts, and architects are not even the most obviously disadvantaged: form an orderly queue behind single mothers, most pensioners and those on disability benefits.

It's true that we are governed by people who don't like architects. Michael Gove, Secretary of State for Education, says that architects have made themselves rich designing lavish schools. No one in this room, he said, preaching to the converted in the shape of a group of Free School aspirants, wants to make architects any richer. Naturally, that empty warehouse, that past-its-sell-by-date department store, that empty drill hall, that will do nicely for our school. Instead, we'll spend all the funds on teachers. Sounds fine, except that no one asked the teachers what the children's attention span might be towards the end of a day spent in under-insulated, overheated classrooms with next-to-no daylight. The Free Schools budgets are not that lavish despite the millions of pounds saved abandoning the well-intentioned but not well-implemented ambition to update every secondary school in England. New Labour's Building Schools for the Future programme was a one-size-fits-all (and therefore inefficient) solution to a complex historical problem. Free Schools are one size fits very few, those few being a young educational elite whose parents are prepared to sign them up to an experiment that even Mrs Thatcher at her most Thatcherite would not have condoned. It's like trying to solve all the problems of the NHS with a handful of private hospitals that are prepared to share their facilities with NHS patients. (Incidentally, we have some of those already, and one very good one. CircleBath won an RIBA Award this year and was considered for the Stirling shortlist; see p. 149. We also have free schools already; they're called independent schools, but that's another story.) The point is that architecture is not a matter of faith but of fact. Money invested in good design is not wasted, whereas building without good design almost certainly is a waste of money.

At a recent meeting between Michael Gove and the RIBA – they are still talking, even if the government doesn't always appear to be listening – the Secretary of State said to the RIBA Chief Executive, Harry Rich, 'You're not telling me, Harry, that if you won the Lottery you wouldn't buy yourself a splendid Queen Anne mansion.' Harry replied, 'That's exactly what I'm saying. I'd find myself a good architect and build a fine modern home in the finest possible setting that would work fantastically for my life in the twenty-first century.' Gove looked at Rich as if he either were slightly mad or couldn't possibly mean this. Such is the gulf today.

The previous government's habit of peppering its pronouncements with the word 'design' almost as much as with the word 'new' was annoying, especially because it seemed to think that good design grows on trees and so doesn't need to be paid for. Cool Britannia may now seem as long ago as the swinging sixties, but at least there is an architectural legacy and one that should prove more lasting than the sink estates. During those early Blair years it seemed as if there had been a societal shift in which most people no longer appeared to have a knee-jerk reaction to modern architecture, that reaction being, as Göring almost said, 'When I hear the word architecture, I reach for my revolver' (the word he actually used was 'culture', and for me this constitutes the most chilling quotation of the last century). However, at a recent party I attended, people – people I know – were saying much the same thing: modern equals awful, high-rise equals terrible. Prince Charles is fighting back, or maybe he never went away; he is certainly finding his voice again. Perhaps the Chelsea Barracks victory – a trouncing of high modernism if ever there was one, albeit modernism represented by a scheme that was probably not going to be Richard Rogers's masterpiece – has given him fresh confidence, leading him to wonder aloud through his acolytes at the lack of classical architecture in London's Olympic Park. Dash it, the Olympics were invented by classical types, so surely … As a matter of fact, the last Olympics with classically inspired architecture were the Berlin games of 1936. Since then the Olympics particularly and Germany generally have steered clear of classicism on account of its rather undeserved connotations. Undeserved, because we should not transfer the epithet of classical orders so as to imply military or political order. And, although we do not have to go as far as Quinlan Terry in seeing classicism as God-given, there is beauty in symmetry. It is more a question of appropriateness. A classical stadium would certainly have worked well, and there have been excellent precedents, but a classical aquatics centre or a classical velodrome? We would have been denied two very different and very beautiful buildings if Charles had had his way. There is a freedom of expression in modernism today that leads to very diverse buildings being designed in its name, some very good, some very bad. Modernism – add the wishful prefix 'late', if you will – has become not a style but a language, like English. And, like English, it has taken over much of the world. It is what most architects speak. It does not mean that the constructs they form are necessarily any good; they are building blocks, no more. We should be fighting for the quality of the product, not fighting about the design of its components. It has taken David Chipperfield to show not only the Germans but also the world the merits of classical proportions and the dangers of asymmetry for asymmetry's sake. (see pp. 32–35).

Recessions can be good for architecture. Architects cannot all be building masterpieces all the time; the world needs background stuff every bit as much. Recessions allow for thought and consideration. Architecture requires ideas, and during a boom there is not enough time for them to be worked out. In the last recession, in the late 1980s and early 1990s, architects had plenty of time on their hands. The likes of Tony Fretton, David Chipperfield, Caruso St John and

Olympic Stadium, Olympic Park, London E15, by Populous

Museum of Modern Literature, Marbach am Neckar, Germany, by David Chipperfield Architects

St Patrick's Catholic Primary School Library and Music Room, London NW5, by Coffey Architects

Ian Ritchie – if there is any 'like' about it – were able to stop and think about where modernism had got to, about its successes and failures. They were able to think about texture, richness and context – all the things that give twenty-first-century architecture its particular character and non-didactic qualities. As these pages show, architecture has seldom been as varied as it is today, and there is much for all those interested in the subject, Prince Charles included.

The best and probably the worst architecture is doubtless still getting constructed; it is the middle ground that is more patchily built upon. And we should worry about the lack of the ordinary. It is, after all, the background to our lives: workplaces, schools, hospitals, housing. We have all but given up on trying to build housing, as if it were some kind of dispensable luxury instead of an inalienable right. That is why, for the third time, this book includes the winners of the annual Housing Design Awards. These awards have always set out to praise and implicitly shame house-builders, in that they measure the success of built schemes in the light of the ambition of their projects. Another kind of house is rewarded through the RIBA Manser Medal. Here, too, the main idea has been to highlight good ideas that might be taken up by house-builders. This year's winner teaches another important lesson in tough times, namely that the most sustainable thing we can do with our housing stock is not automatically to knock it down and start again, but to upgrade the existing fabric or structure, making it more energy-efficient and better suited to today's family life (see pp. 79–80). It is also (Mr Gove, please note) a good example of an architect practising what he preaches.

Meanwhile, the Stephen Lawrence Prize reminds us that society had been fragile, if not broken, long before 2010 or even 1997, but it also shows that even small budgets can be used to tackle the problem. This was a message that interested the BBC, which agreed to include the award in its TV coverage of the Stirling dinner and also, for the first time, the RIBA's main international prize, the Lubetkin, thus demonstrating to a large audience that architecture is not all about glossy projects, but nor is it merely parochial. British architecture continues to play its part on the international stage – a role that is increasingly important when work is hard to come by at home.

This book again includes the student winners of the President's Medals. These talented students are the future of architecture, and it is unlikely that they at least will be lost to the profession, if only because of the attention that winning such prizes draws towards them and their work. David Adjaye and Sean Griffiths of FAT (Fashion Architecture Taste) are past winners of President's Medals, as is Simon Hudspith, the father of Jack, this year's Bronze Medallist. Simon's fine housing in Southwark was this year considered for the Stirling shortlist (see p. 163). There is a pattern of excellence here that is embodied in the RIBA's awards, and it is to be hoped that it is an auspicious one. Housing and architecture in general need the kind of ideas present both in Simon's courtyard housing and in Jack's scheme for a cookery school in the ruins of a Scottish Roman fort.

Each year the RIBA brings together the Bronze, Silver and Dissertation Medal winners with the Royal Gold Medallist. This year Sir David Chipperfield gave a measured critique of the students' work, telling them, 'You are in a special place as a student to develop passions and enthusiasms; you are not there to solve real problems. The challenge in architecture is to make poetry out of the mundane.'

The Gold Medal represents the pinnacle of achievement in international professional practice, a recognition that Chipperfield, with typical modesty, did not feel he deserved. The student medals represent the seeds for the growth of the profession. At a time when architecture is hard hit by recession, by ill-wishers in high places, by procurement methods that often place cost above value, it needs to hang on to its principal tenets: the quality of its education, the integrity of its practitioners and the originality of its thinking. This book represents the latest attempts in that struggle.

THE BIG CONVERSATION
ANGELA BRADY, RIBA PRESIDENT

There are so many architectural awards these days that one needs to scrutinize the criteria of the award, the awarding body and the judges to see if one can have faith in the outcome. Is the award for glitzy architecture that will be out of fashion in ten years' time, or for a building that will have true and lasting value to the community in which it sits? At a time when we need to wean ourselves off oil and come up with super-efficient buildings, is the award for the best low-carbon building? Are we examining the look of a building from the outside, or its functionality? Are we engaging the public enough in our judgements, since the projects will affect them most of all, or are we relying overly on peer opinion, which many say is limited and introverted and does not give the real picture? In short, are we rewarding the right things in the right way?

Too often 'awards' are created for the sake of publicity, and are a way of gathering people together over an expensive dinner to dish out prizes that are not worth the paper on which they are printed, or that are for projects without any merit.

Awards can only ever be a snapshot of the times in which they are made, and some are literally judged on photographs of buildings, meaning that clever photography can hide the errors. The RIBA Awards visit all buildings under consideration, and those shortlisted for the Stirling Prize are visited by three panels of expert judges. I have just completed this last task, and I must say that getting personal tours around some of the finest buildings in the United Kingdom and overseas is one of the delights of being the RIBA President.

I have seen awards from all sides, as I have been a member of the public, a client, an architecture award-winner and a judge, and have been vice-chair of the Civic Trust Awards for six years. The best awards, I think, are those for which the rules of entry and evaluation are clear, and that include a visit to the buildings by a team of experts and lay people who are unbiased and balanced in their views, perceptions and evaluation.

Architecture and the spaces around us have a profound effect on how we feel and behave, and on how we develop as individuals and as a community. As RIBA President, I intend to work on increasing the public's and politicians' understanding of the value that well-designed buildings bring to people's lives, and on helping to bring about the necessary political and educational changes that will enable the delivery of the best possible sustainable built environment.

So I will do all I can to advance the causes of architecture and architects, at a time when, I believe, society urgently needs our skills and vision as never before. Why are architects needed? Both visibly and invisibly, our society is changing. The wider economic environment is driving a reduction in public spending, and the reconfiguration of funding strategies is causing major upheavals.

We have seen the scrapping of the Building Schools for the Future programme, with architects wrongly cited as major contributors to its failure. We have had civil unrest that, when its origins are mapped, can be traced back to significant blocks of social housing, where the so-called 'feral' society sought by the Prime Minister, David Cameron, may well be found. But we should be clear that while the issues identified by Cameron as evidence of a 'broken society' have been many years in the making, this is no reason to delay much-needed change. As architects, we need to be at the centre of that change, in partnership with all who share our aspirations.

I have been a campaigner all my life. I have been involved in campaigns to save loved buildings, and I have fought for a more diverse profession. I have championed better-designed buildings, and sat on some of the best advisory panels in the United Kingdom. I used to be quite critical of the RIBA, and twelve years ago I asked what the institute was doing about equality in the profession. With so few women architects – just 9 per cent at the time – we needed a platform. Two weeks later I was invited to chair Women in Architecture, part of the new Architects for Change group of dedicated RIBA members. We campaigned for a more equal and diverse profession by promoting the best women and the best black and ethnic-minority architects. Today women make up 18 per cent of the profession, but still only 2 per cent of architects come from black, Asian and minority ethnic communities. The current economic climate, and the lack of education funding and job opportunities, continue to put obstacles in the way of progress.

Another way in which we can help to raise architectural standards is by holding more competitions to bring about the best designs. We need to give younger members an opportunity to win the chance to design projects that would not otherwise come their way for twenty years, if ever. We also need to ensure that architects are paid a fee for the work they do in entering these competitions. This will attract both new practices and the more experienced. Some of our best architects found early recognition of their ideas through winning competitions; Richard Rogers's design for the Pompidou Centre is just one good example.

But we need to help the next generation of architects at an even earlier stage in their careers. We can link our practices with some of the forty-four schools of architecture, we can share research, and we can make the curriculum for architectural education more relevant to practice and so make the crossover more rewarding and less painful.

The government's new and simplified system for a 'National Planning Policy Framework' aims to give people a say in what gets built in their area, but only if they set up a 'Local Plan' in time. If they do not, six months later there could be a free-for-all for developers, who control huge swathes of land and need adhere only to a 'presumption in favour of sustainable development' – whatever that means. There are still huge unresolved issues in relation to Local Plans. We need to engage the public, encourage them to demand better design and empower them to rebuild their communities. This is an unrivalled opportunity for architects to adopt a leadership role within local communities and really make a difference.

The economic collapse of recent years has had a devastating effect on architecture and the construction industry as a whole, with many architects and fellow professionals facing unemployment, under-employment or shelved projects. As part of our recovery, we must work even more collaboratively to reduce waste and produce better, more affordable and more sustainable buildings. The government can support us by ensuring short-term cost-saving decisions are not made to the detriment of our longer-term health, homes, education and prosperity.

As regards procurement, we need to remove the obstacles that prevent architects from producing quality buildings of value. The tick-box mentality of local authorities and European Union procurement is hugely wasteful of time and talent, and puts more importance on perceived risk than on design, value and sustainability. The bane of my professional life as a practitioner in private practice is procurement. In common with 90 per cent of all architectural practices, my firm consists of fewer than ten people, yet the projects that we are all skilled at doing are mostly out of our reach, because of this lazy system. One of my first tasks is to lobby the government and the EU for better procurement that gives everyone fair access to projects. We need more design and less box-ticking.

That said, I have ticked a few boxes myself in my time. A few ago years, not many people would have predicted that an Irish woman would be President of the RIBA – I certainly didn't. Bringing architecture to the public is very important. I want the public to love architecture and our environment, so that they will come to see sustainable buildings as a basic human need, and demand much more from architects and politicians. Our built environment is too important and too fragile for us to make mistakes that will last a lifetime. Our lives are shaped by our built environment, and much depends on us getting it right.

The RIBA is one of the most respected institutes in the world, and, as its new leader, I want members to take pride in their efforts to build a better environment. The awards process is just one way in which to reward achievement in the built environment. However, the true merit of buildings and whether they are worthy of an award is demonstrated by the test of time and the feedback of the clients and the users. And I hope that, by this time next year, the RIBA will be able to announce an award that does just that: revisits previous award-winning buildings, talks to their users and assesses whether the projects have measured up to their architects' aspirations. With such an award, the RIBA will be leading the way – as it has done consistently during the past two centuries.

THE RIBA STIRLING PRIZE
IN ASSOCIATION WITH *THE ARCHITECTS' JOURNAL*
AND KINGSPAN BENCHMARK

The RIBA Stirling Prize, now in its sixteenth year, is sponsored by *The Architects' Journal* and Kingspan Benchmark. It is awarded to the architects of the building thought to be the most significant for the evolution of architecture and the built environment. A building is eligible for the prize if it is in the United Kingdom or elsewhere in the European Union and is designed by a practice with a principal office in the UK. The shortlist is selected from RIBA Award-winners, and the winner receives £20,000 and a trophy designed by Morag Myerscough. The prize is named after the architect Sir James Stirling (1926–1992), one of the most important architects of his generation and a progressive thinker and designer throughout his career.

The key criterion for any award given by the RIBA is that the project should demonstrate excellence. RIBA Awards juries should assess design excellence irrespective of style, size or complexity of project. They should take into account constraints of budget, brief and timetable, and be sensitive to the economic and social contexts of each project. Juries are required to judge what they see, not what they, as architects, might have done with a similar brief. They should also understand that almost all buildings, even great works of architecture, have some flaws.

Juries are asked to judge the quality of the design of the scheme, particularly in respect of: the budget; the spatial experience that the scheme offers; the complexity of brief and degree of difficulty – the scheme's architectural ambition and ideas; its design vision; the selection and detailing of materials; the extent of innovation, invention and originality; the contract type; the appropriateness of the scheme's structural and servicing systems; fitness for purpose and the level of client satisfaction; the scheme's response to the issues of accessibility and sustainability and other social factors; its capacity to stimulate, engage and delight its occupants and visitors. An award-winning project should be capable of enduring as a fine work of architecture throughout its working life.

For previous winners of the prize, see p. 245.

WINNER

EVELYN GRACE ACADEMY
SHAKESPEARE ROAD, LONDON SE24
ZAHA HADID ARCHITECTS

SHORTLIST

AN GAELÁRAS
DERRY
O'DONNELL + TUOMEY

THE ANGEL BUILDING
ST JOHN STREET, LONDON N1
ALLFORD HALL MONAGHAN MORRIS

MUSEUM FOLKWANG
ESSEN, GERMANY
DAVID CHIPPERFIELD ARCHITECTS

ROYAL SHAKESPEARE
AND SWAN THEATRES
STRATFORD-UPON-AVON
BENNETTS ASSOCIATES

THE VELODROME
OLYMPIC PARK, LONDON E15
HOPKINS ARCHITECTS

JUDGES

ANGELA BRADY
RIBA PRESIDENT
RIBA President 2011–13 and a director of Brady Mallalieu Architects. A founder member of RIBA Architects for Change and former chair of Women in Architecture, she promotes the value of good design through appearances on Channel 4's *Home Show*, and through schools and public workshops.

ALISON BROOKS
ARCHITECT
Director of Alison Brooks Architects, which was one of three practices to share the Stirling Prize in 2008 for Accordia in Cambridge. She was selected to participate in the Audi Urban Future Award in 2010, and her work was shown at the Architecture Biennale in Venice in the same year. Brooks teaches at the Architectural Association in London and internationally.

SIR PETER COOK
ARCHITECT
Co-founder of the radical architectural group Archigram, which was awarded the RIBA's highest award, the Royal Gold Medal, in 2002. A former director of the Institute of Contemporary Arts, London, and the Bartlett, University College London, he continues to practise across Europe.

HANIF KARA
STRUCTURAL ENGINEER
Structural engineer and co-founder of AKT II, which has engineered 180 award-winning projects, including Peckham Library and Media Centre, London, the Stirling Prize-winning project in 2000. He has served as a CABE commissioner and a juror for the Aga Khan Award, and teaches at the Architectural Association in London and at Harvard University.

DAN PEARSON
LANDSCAPE DESIGNER
A landscape and garden designer with an international reputation for planting excellence, an intuitive approach to the organization of space, and the practice of sustainable design. He trained at the RHS Garden Wisley and the Royal Botanic Gardens, Kew, before establishing the Dan Pearson Studio in 1987.

EVELYN GRACE ACADEMY
SHAKESPEARE ROAD, LONDON SE24

ZAHA HADID ARCHITECTS

CLIENT: ARK SCHOOLS
STRUCTURAL ENGINEER: ARUP
CONTRACTOR: MACE PLUS
CONTRACT VALUE: £37,500,000
DATE OF COMPLETION: 2010
GROSS INTERNAL AREA: 10,745 SQ. M
IMAGES: LUKE HAYES – VIEW (BOTTOM; OPPOSITE, TOP; P. 21; P. 22; P. 23);
        HUFTON & CROW – VIEW (P. 17; OPPOSITE, BOTTOM; P. 20)

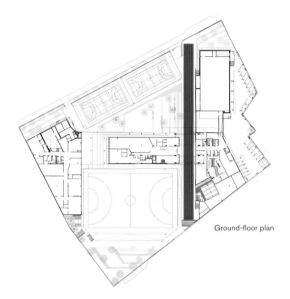

Ground-floor plan

Evelyn Grace is a truly extraordinary and original school, but in the opinion of the Stirling judges it is not a one-off. Architecture should not be about replicability, because it leads to one-size-fits-all solutions. There are, however, lessons aplenty to be learned from this scheme.

The architect received a complex brief: four schools under a single academy umbrella, with the need to express both unity and independence. This is a large academy (for 1100 pupils) on a small site (just 1.4 hectares instead of the average 8 hectares). Without the luxury of a large greenfield site on which to scatter four discrete schools, the architect has opted for what is called stacking-and-packing, yet because of the

generosity of the accommodation and the ample provision of daylight in most areas, it does not feel that way.

This is narrative architecture that tells the story of the city, the neighbourhood and its student community as one moves through the site. Bringing renewed life to a long-neglected street, Zaha Hadid announces the new school with a ribbon of structural concrete that pulls away dynamically from the site edge, offering to the gritty surroundings a foreground oasis of landscaping and playing fields. Having attracted our attention, she leads us inside, where the architecture really starts to happen. Being a star architect allows a degree of licence, and Hadid has used her reputation entirely for good, challenging our expectations of what makes excellent academy architecture. For instance, there is no sign of the atrium that has become a trope in the design of so many academies. Instead, the money has wisely been spent on well-designed and lit classrooms, wide corridors (the best the judges had ever seen in a school), robust concrete elements and high-quality finishes to doors, ceilings and internal fixtures. The quality of the cladding and the internal glazed partitions is exceptional, and these will prove their cost-effectiveness over many years of use by 1000-plus students per day. The airy,

flexible hall on two floors at the heart of the plan can be divided by acoustic screens into dining, teaching, assembly, drama and indoor-sport areas.

Curiously for a school that specializes in sport, the original site seemingly lacked any opportunity for significant outdoor sport, but the architect has responded with guile and intelligence, providing a multi-use Astroturf pitch that can be used for football or simultaneously by games requiring smaller playing areas. From an upper outdoor terrace one has clear views into the double gymnasium, kitted out with university-quality equipment. This is a cathedral-like space compared to most school gyms, filled with natural light from a great north wall of glazing that follows stairs down to the playing fields.

The two entrances to the site are joined by a bright-red 100-metre sprint track. The academy bridges the track at the 50-metre point, marking the doors in a playful, light-hearted manner. Why not make a running track an exciting landscape device for a school entrance?

The two upper storeys of the school buildings rise out of a podium, which appears to reduce their height and mass in this area of small-scale housing. The podium roof also provides

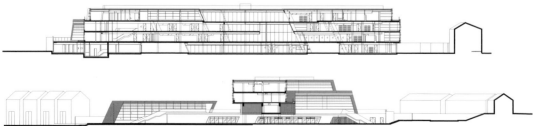

Sections

Third-floor plan

terraces that act as distinct gathering spaces for each school and age group in the morning and during breaks, thus reducing the bullying that inevitably occurs when children of different ages are forced together.

Internally, the academy is a good-quality and functional modern school, with well-judged exciting spatial moments as reminders that this is architecture and not just building: a fine stair detail here; a lovingly placed window mid-way up a stair there; benches designed into nooks and crannies; walls made of lockers, adding dabs of colour to the grey-and-white palette and opening on to corridors; with glazed clerestories allowing natural classroom light to fill the corridors. None of this is in any way at the expense of utility or value.

The Stirling judges all agreed that the Evelyn Grace Academy establishes principles for future school-building: ultra-robust construction, a compact site strategy and excellent integrated landscaping, demonstrating the highest level of design for this neighbourhood. It has ingenious internal planning, uplifting spaces distributed throughout the building and beautifully designed internal sports facilities. This well-designed scheme encourages children to run into school in the morning: what finer endorsement could there be than that?

AN GAELÁRAS
DERRY

O'DONNELL + TUOMEY

CLIENT: AN GAELÁRAS
STRUCTURAL ENGINEER: ALBERT FRY ASSOCIATES
SERVICES ENGINEER: IN2 ENGINEERING
CONTRACTOR: JPM CONTRACTS
CONTRACT VALUE: £2,800,000
DATE OF COMPLETION: SEPTEMBER 2009
GROSS INTERNAL AREA: 1980 SQ. M
IMAGES: ALICE CLANCY (P. 26); DENNIS GILBERT – VIEW (TOP; BOTTOM;
    OPPOSITE; P. 27)

An Gaeláras is a cultural centre that promotes the use and enjoyment of the Irish language and its culture. In Northern Ireland there is no such thing as just a building, and this one more than most is grounded in the thirty years of Troubles that beset this part of the island of Ireland. It was funded by twenty different bodies north and south of the border, with money from both governments. Even so, funds were tight, and this has led to an inventiveness on the part of the architect, who revels in a richness of detail and colour.

Faced with an almost impossible landlocked site in a street of Georgian and Victorian terraces, further compromised by an electricity substation that occupies a third of the frontage and a

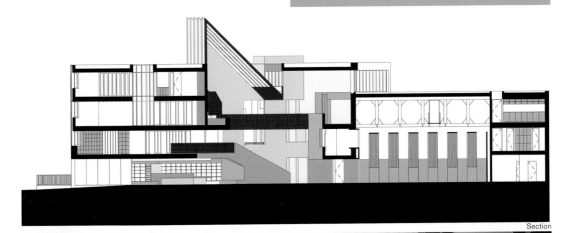

Section

fire exit that takes up another quarter, the architect has devised an intriguing and intricate vortex plan. With only one external elevation, three internal façades have been created. Lots of architects talk about creating 'streets'; O'Donnell + Tuomey really has. Inside the cranked space, which is lit by a large, steeply sloping rooflight, it is as if one were in a twisting medieval lane in the old city. Shops, cafes and bars are all here and lead through to a theatre. At every turn joy, inventiveness and a sense of pleasure may be found in the detailed exploration of form, light and materiality.

Above, teaching and office spaces, linked by a series of stairs, bridges and platforms that circle and cross the internal courtyard, jostle for views. It is like exploring a castle, with secret staircases and surprising bolt-holes. The stairs appear and disappear as the route unfolds, making visitors want to explore and drawing them up both visually and physically to the upper levels. It is a veritable architectural playground. The plan appears haphazard, but in fact it fixes places and connections, and the success of An Gaeláras lies in its ability to house all the different functions within spaces that have adequate light and views. Up on the roof there is potential aplenty. A round of budget cuts put paid to the planned offices at this level, leaving the empty canvas of a roof terrace.

The single elevation has suffered somewhat at the hands of the planners. The architect's idea was for a set of three bays, two of them angled to look up and down the street, the third to face directly across the street. Sadly these were rejected on the grounds that the tone of the street is Georgian flat-fronted. (Precedence did not, unfortunately, stop planners from giving permission for a dull Georgian pastiche with UPVC windows next door.) Instead, the architect has cleverly inverted the bays so that nothing projects beyond the building line, yet an interesting zig-zag appearance has been retained as you see the frontage from afar, making for an intriguing piece of streetscape. As for that substation, it is elegantly hidden by a dull-red steel screen (to match the interior steelwork) and looks like a bottle store.

In scale, the building respects its neighbours, but materially it is very different and speaks of culture as something that is aspirational as well as communal. The sense of the building as a sculptural intervention in a conventional street is enhanced by the use of beautiful board-marked concrete. The concrete adds gravitas and allows for the use of cheaper materials elsewhere: plywood, composition board and painted plaster.

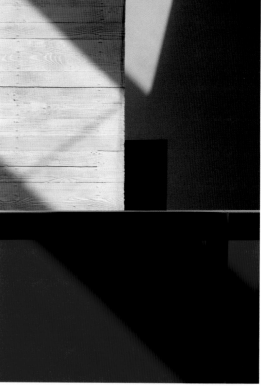

An Gaeláras uses dynamic plan form to break down convention and enhance the sense of community. The organization and the aesthetics complement each other to produce a rigorous piece of architecture that characterizes the institution instead of merely reflecting the predilections of the architect. It is a vital, ingenious and energetic scheme that can generate and absorb a lot of the energy of the people who use it. It has been thoughtfully put together as a series of fractured spaces that draw the visitor into and up through the building – so much so that users have been found making themselves at home in offices, thinking them public rooms, plucking books from shelves and being reluctant to move on. That is an unusual mark of good architecture and of a highly user-friendly building.

THE ANGEL BUILDING
ST JOHN STREET, LONDON N1

ALLFORD HALL MONAGHAN MORRIS

CLIENT: DERWENT LONDON
STRUCTURAL ENGINEER: ADAMS KARA TAYLOR
SERVICES ENGINEER: NORMAN DISNEY & YOUNG
CONTRACTOR: BAM CONSTRUCTION UK
CONTRACT VALUE: £72,000,000
DATE OF COMPLETION: OCTOBER 2010
GROSS INTERNAL AREA: 33,224 SQ. M
IMAGES: LEE MAWDSLEY (P. 30 BOTTOM); TIMOTHY SOAR (TOP; BOTTOM;
    OPPOSITE; P. 30 TOP; P. 31)

This speculative office space redefines the sector. An
unremarkable 1980s office block has been transformed into
a building of elegance and poise that has created new interiors
of great refinement, and also contributes positively to life on the
streets outside.

A new tailored façade to St John Street sweeps round the
corner with Pentonville Road, connecting with the set-back
building line established by a neo-Georgian neighbour and
creating a new landscaped strip (designed by J. & L. Gibbons)
that is refreshingly simple and uncluttered – and, unlike so much
public space today, does not make the mistake of being all about
hard landscaping. Here there has been no fear of greenery, and
the planting and the shimmering trees form a foil to the crisp lines
of the new façades and help to aerate this busy part of Islington.

The architect has moved the entrance from the obvious
corner position to one midway along the long façade. The slope
of the street means that the entry sequence is raked to meet the
existing ground floor, adding drama and a sense of arrival. The new
building retains the original structure while infilling an old courtyard

and adding new office girth on two edges. The additional floor-space (there is now 25,000 square metres of lettable space instead of the original 15,000 square metres) is the key to increasing the building's rental value, unlocking the development. Retail units – including a Jamie Oliver restaurant that spills out on to a paved outdoor area – are incorporated into the ground floor on St John Street.

The openness of the building produces an ambience that is quite different from that of most commercial buildings in the City of London. The entry sequence, with a publicly accessible cafe and lounge (the security is provided by smartly dressed people, not machines), sets civilized new standards for ways in which the atrium form can be used to animate a commercial ground floor as well as simply letting light in. A finely executed and generous 3-metre grid of *in-situ* concrete fins and beams (instead of the usual enslaving 1.5 metres) rises up to a gridded top-light. The colour and the smooth surface of the concrete are complemented by the smaller-scale grid of a delicate terrazzo floor inspired by a floor in Carlo Scarpa's Olivetti building in Milan. A magnificent polished black sculptural piece by McChesney Architects, *Out of the Strong Came Forth Sweetness*, looks like thick black treacle poured from the back of a spoon. It adds drama and counterpoint to the Kahnian gravitas of the atrium.

The whole building uses a limited colour palette, ranging from black to white through any number of shades of grey; the richness is in the detailing, in the furniture and the materials. The top storey opens out on to a roof terrace of such generous proportions and with such good fixtures and fittings that it has the feel of a luxury hotel, not a commercial office. All that is missing is an infinity pool. But then Derwent is no ordinary client. A past winner of the RIBA's Client of the Year (in 2007), the firm knows that good tenants will be prepared to pay for high-quality buildings that perform well.

The offices as offered to those tenants have no suspended ceilings, so that the thermal mass of the concrete is fully available. Displacement ventilation is supplied through vents in the floor and drawn out through high-level concealed grilles. A rainwater-harvesting system produces the water for irrigation of the landscape and for flushing the toilets, saving the equivalent of almost half a million flushes a year – although the gents' urinals are waterless. This building is all about performance, but the most sustainable aspect of the project is the retention of the previous structure's concrete frame, which accounts for a massive saving of CO_2 and reduced the budget by £350 per square metre.

It is to the huge credit of Derwent London and its architect, AHMM, that they have created such high-end speculative office space and let it so successfully in a time of recession. The project is extremely well made and resolved, offering an idea of how building and working in the city might become a more dignified act.

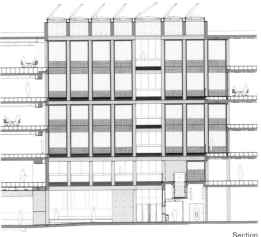

Section

MUSEUM FOLKWANG
ESSEN, GERMANY

DAVID CHIPPERFIELD ARCHITECTS

CLIENT: NEUBAU MUSEUM FOLKWANG ESSEN ON BEHALF OF THE ALFRIED
    KRUPP VON BOHLEN UND HALBACH-STIFTUNG
STRUCTURAL ENGINEERS/CONTRACTORS: PÜHL UND BECKER
    INGENIEURBERATUNG; SERONEIT UND SCHNEIDER
SERVICES ENGINEER: GIESEN-GILLHOFF-LOOMANS
CONTRACT VALUE: CONFIDENTIAL
DATE OF COMPLETION: APRIL 2010
GROSS INTERNAL AREA: 24,800 SQ. M
IMAGES: CHRISTIAN RICHTERS – VIEW

Museum Folkwang (the name derives from that of Norse
mythology's gathering place of the dead) is a breathtakingly
accomplished design. The brief was simple: to provide a home
to match in architectural terms the artistic quality of one of
Germany's best collections of twentieth-century art. A
predecessor museum was badly bombed in the Second World
War, and reopened in 1960; ever since then, the museum has
been a meeting room for the city as well as home to a world-
class collection of nineteenth- and twentieth-century art. Thanks
to the transparency of the late-1950s building, passers-by on the
street and even people sitting in their homes have been able to
admire the artworks. David Chipperfield's new and impressive
building continues that democratic tradition with understated
elegance and beauty.

    Chipperfield (the recipient of this year's Royal Gold Medal;
see pp. 196–203) won the international competition for the

Floor plan

Section

project in 2007, and the building opened in time for Essen to become European Capital of Culture in 2010. It continues the architectural principles of the 1950s scheme and develops them, much as a jazz musician might riff on the tune of a classic number. The existing museum was in a beautifully simple Miesian building designed by the city architects, and allowed people passing by in the street to see the Van Goghs. Unfortunately, it had been extended in the 1980s by a building that had dated quickly and worn badly. The benefactor who funded its replacement was a friend of Mies van der Rohe, so the new project is doubly appropriate.

The major move by Chipperfield was deciding on a podium to level off the sloping site and form the stone base for the new buildings, which replace and match the footprint of the 1980s museum, while retaining the 1950s building. The result is a rather grand approach from the city via a series of ramps and staircases. Inside are genuinely uplifting, light-filled public spaces, offering a serene yet mesmeric mixture of inward-looking courtyards and external views out. These are almost entirely grassed – immaculate and dazzling greenswards untouched by human feet and rolled out right up to the building line like a carpet. They feature a minimal number of specimen trees, which cast shadows on to the translucent glass, so that from the inside they appear as moving Japanese sketches.

The major external cladding is of large panels of crushed recycled glass, giving a shimmering translucent finish that has more of the qualities of alabaster than of glass. Carefully detailed top-lighting systems blend natural and artificial light in galleries

that are capable of being completely blacked out. The museum's director wanted natural light even at the cost of unevenness: for him changes of light are preferable to a series of perfectly lit rooms. He has those in abundance in the 1950s galleries, where the preponderance of artificial light casts a yellow hue across the collections. In the large, flexible temporary exhibition space, the lighting grid has been coordinated with a bespoke flexible but highly stable partitioning system that can easily be demounted and reassembled to meet the requirements for each show.

If anything, the client has shown the architecture a little too much respect, with the spacious light-filled entrance hall all but innocent of art, and instead conceived as an open interior courtyard with a cafe, restaurant and bookshop. Within the galleries the hanging is also understated, but it does allow for quiet contemplation of what is a breathtaking collection. In addition, the scheme comprises a library and reading room, a multifunctional hall, lavishly daylit restoration workshops, and art stores for the iceberg-like hidden four-fifths of the collection.

Museum Folkwang was described by no less an authority than Paul J. Sachs, art historian and co-founder of the Museum of Modern Art in New York, as 'the most beautiful museum in the world'. That was in 1932. The following year the Nazis came to power, and much of the Museum Folkwang's 'degenerate' art was sold off, appropriated or even burned. In all, no fewer than 1400 pieces were lost, only a handful of which were ever returned. Once again, in the early part of the twenty-first century, the museum is living up to its billing, thanks to the skill and inspiration of David Chipperfield and his Berlin team.

ROYAL SHAKESPEARE
AND SWAN THEATRES
STRATFORD-UPON-AVON

BENNETTS ASSOCIATES

CLIENT: PETER WILSON, ROYAL SHAKESPEARE COMPANY
STRUCTURAL ENGINEER: BURO HAPPOLD
THEATRE CONSULTANT: CHARCOALBLUE
CONTRACTOR: MACE
CONTRACT VALUE: £60,000,000
DATE OF COMPLETION: NOVEMBER 2010
GROSS INTERNAL AREA: 12,000 SQ. M
IMAGES: PETER COOK – VIEW
ROYAL SHAKESPEARE COMPANY WAS WINNER OF THE RIBA CLIENT OF
    THE YEAR

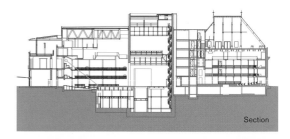

Section

In Stratford-upon-Avon, the relationship between theatre and
town has long been fraught, in the same way that town and gown
divide in Oxford and Cambridge. Local feeling put paid to Erick
van Egeraat's highly individualistic attempt in 1998 to replace
Elisabeth Scott's 1930s theatre in its idyllic Avon-side setting.
Instead the council listed her Art Deco façades and foyers,
according them Grade II* status. The new brief then called for the
rebuilding of the larger theatre to form a new 1000-seat thrust-
stage auditorium, plus new facilities for actors and audience, all
within an urban masterplan.

In this flat, low-lying town the faceted tower works as both
marker and viewing platform, and it brings into the theatre people

Elevation

who would not have thought of going to see a play. Many of them are intrigued by the place and end up booking tickets. But the tower also makes a historic reference. The old Victorian theatre featured a tower of identical height, the purpose of which was not viewing but fire-fighting. Sadly, the massive head-tank it contained did not stop the fire that destroyed most of the building and led to Scott's flawed masterpiece.

When Scott designed her theatre, Art Deco and cinema were twin design beacons. The former has left a number of rooms that have been lovingly restored and sympathetically fitted. The influence of the latter led to a wide fan-shaped auditorium with acoustics the actors had to fight. That has changed utterly. Bennetts retained the rear wall, however, and this move has produced the most successful part of the scheme: the carefully crafted spaces in the voids between the back wall of the old theatre and the back wall of the new one, which are used for creative projection as well as circulation. A small row of seats remains in place on the retained wall to show just how far from the stage the back seats used to be: 27 metres, as opposed to today's 15 metres.

Some of the best theatre results from improvisation, and this building has the feeling of being developed in much the same way: detailed research, endless debate and argument, experimentation and inspiration, fine-tuning and honing. As the theatre designer puts it, theatre is best when it is kept messy and historical and is not clinical and refined. This theatre is true to that spirit, but Bennetts has brought his modernist instincts to the mix. This is best seen in the way the curved, glazed addition of a restaurant peers over the Art Deco parapet; in the strict, almost industrial, order of the dressing-room wing that gives every actor river views; and in the broad sweep of a new foyer that links the two theatres and across which scenery is trundled through massive doors on to the stage. This is a real working theatre, not a precious one.

The new thrust-stage auditorium works extraordinarily well. It is robust, even rough. Its feel is a bit like the Globe Theatre's in London, and it has an exciting atmosphere. As in the case of the tower, it is historic in its references and contemporary in its design, and the acoustics are superb. The deep thrust of the stage means that the actors are in among the audience in a very intimate fashion, and the front two rows are in real danger of being squirted with Shakespearean stage gore.

One of the Stirling judges described Bennetts' work as acupuncture, not surgery. The architecture does work from the inside out, and the theatre was only briefly anaesthetized. In that short time when the theatre was necessarily dark, its place was taken by Ian Ritchie's Cor-ten Courtyard Theatre down the road, which acted as an experimental workshop for the architecture of the new theatre. It had a curved auditorium, whereas the new Royal Shakespeare auditorium is faceted; with its high galleries and structural columns it is a theatre that, in the words of the artistic director Michael Boyd, 'Shakespeare might recognize'.

One local told the judges: 'I love the stripped-backness of it, and I love the idea of reusing so many of the materials of the old theatre. They've recycled the boards trodden by Gielgud, Olivier and Richardson in the foyers. You can almost see the blood, the sweat and the tears that went into those old productions.'

THE VELODROME
OLYMPIC PARK, LONDON E15

HOPKINS ARCHITECTS

CLIENT: THE OLYMPIC DELIVERY AUTHORITY
STRUCTURAL ENGINEER: EXPEDITION
SERVICES ENGINEER: BDSP PARTNERSHIP
CONTRACTOR: ISG
CONTRACT VALUE: CONFIDENTIAL
DATE OF COMPLETION: JANUARY 2011
GROSS INTERNAL AREA: 21,700 SQ. M
IMAGES: RICHARD DAVIES (TOP; OPPOSITE; P. 42); MARTIN KEOGH (P. 43)

Located at the north end of the Olympic Park masterplan in east London, the Velodrome exudes elegance and simplicity. The very shape of the building signals the track itself, a continuous, sinuous form that seems to pre-empt and explain the movement of the event.

The site was a rubbish tip for the area of West Ham, and was referred to by the architect as Fridge Mountain. The mountain remains (this is the highest point of the Olympic Park and a fitting platform for the majestic, low-slung building), the land remediated and capped by 2 metres of good earth and home now also to a switchback BMX track, a 1.6-kilometre road-cycle circuit, and 6 kilometres of mountain-bike trails. The project's legacy is already assured. And to make locals even happier, once the Olympic Park is open they will be able in perpetuity to come right up to the Velodrome, press their eager faces to the glass of the concourse and watch their cycling heroes in training.

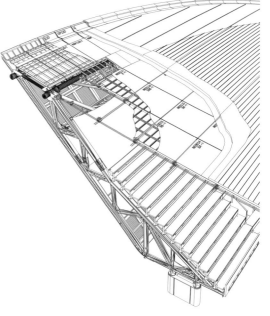

Roof cutaway

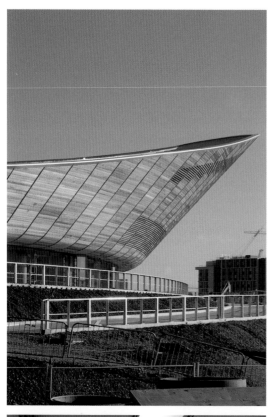

The building is made of three elements: the roof, the concourse and the plinth. The glazing separates the curve of the larch-clad roof soffit and the concrete of the plinth. The approach from the plinth up to the concourse and the arena, via a well-detailed staircase, is modest and low-key, and the drama of the upper space is held back. The material palette is well controlled, and fine *in-situ* concrete abounds. The material and visual emphasis is on the beauty and the colour of the timber track.

The cable-net roof seems to hang in space, detached from the ground by the glazed concourse. While the roof is a significant engineering achievement, it does not shout its presence; instead it is turned through 90 degrees from the track from which it takes its shape, and sits low over the bowl, adding drama and focus to the event itself. The double curve of the roof (which has been likened to a Pringles crisp) is four times stronger than a flat roof would have been. Cable-net structures work like a distorted tennis racket. The frame usually takes the form of a ring beam, but here the building's stiff structure takes the stresses of the roof and transfers them to the ground, hence the lightness of the steel in the roof, with massive savings in embedded energy. The cable net is not so very different from Frei Otto's structure for the 1972 Munich Olympic Stadium, but here the roof has to be opaque to suit the cyclists. So it is clad with 1000 birchwood panels, attached to nodes, and topped with 30 centimetres of insulation and a top layer of rigid Kalzip ringed with a flexible rim of Sarnafil, which channels rainwater into giant hoppers for recycling.

The arena is an extremely intimate space, given the seating capacity of 6000. No seat is very far away from the track; indeed, in places spectators are literally within touching distance of the cyclists – and, if they are at the back, of the roof that comes down to meet them. Cyclists like it hot (28°C brings out the best in them), but spectators prefer somewhat cooler temperatures, so the natural ventilation/heating (powered by a central power plant using biomass) is blown in under the seats and extracted through the roof. Jet nozzles aimed at the track can briefly and quickly heat that area up to the sort of level required by Chris Hoy, winner of three gold medals at the 2008 Beijing Olympics and a judge in the architectural competition for this velodrome. Thanks to its rooflights, the building can operate with no artificial light; only high-definition television cameras require the 2000-lux lighting that will be needed only during the Olympics.

There are no eco-gizmos here, just thoughtful strategies based on pre-existing technologies, resulting in a 32 per cent reduction in overall energy use compared with the requirements of building regulations. The building is pared down like a racing bike and consummately delivers a simple idea, carrying it out beautifully and efficiently at a cost of around £3000 per square metre. It is an enormous credit to both the client and the design team that the effect is one of effortlessness and grace. The plan is an exercise in clarity of purpose and rigorous resolution, while the form is, quite simply, memorable.

THE RIBA
LUBETKIN PRIZE

The RIBA Lubetkin Prize is awarded to the architect of the best RIBA International Award-winning building. Buildings eligible for RIBA International Awards are those outside the European Union designed by RIBA Chartered Architects or RIBA International Fellows.

The prize is named after Berthold Lubetkin (1901–1990), the architect from Georgia who immigrated to Britain in the 1930s and went on to establish the radical architecture group Tecton. He is best known for the two Highpoint buildings in Highgate, London (1933–38), and for the Penguin Pool at London Zoo (1934). The pool provided the inspiration for a cast-bronze plaque designed and made by the artist Petr Weigl. The plaque was presented to the winner of the Lubetkin Prize at the RIBA Stirling Prize Dinner.

For previous winners of the prize, see p. 245.

WINNER

THE MET
BANGKOK, THAILAND
WOHA WITH TANDEM ARCHITECTS
2001

SHORTLIST

GUANGZHOU OPERA HOUSE
GUANGZHOU, GUANGDONG, CHINA
ZAHA HADID ARCHITECTS

MASDAR INSTITUTE OF SCIENCE AND TECHNOLOGY
MASDAR CITY, ABU DHABI, UNITED ARAB EMIRATES
FOSTER + PARTNERS

MUSEUM OF FINE ARTS, BOSTON
BOSTON, MASSACHUSETTS, UNITED STATES
FOSTER + PARTNERS

VIRGINIA MUSEUM OF FINE ARTS
RICHMOND, VIRGINIA, UNITED STATES
RICK MATHER ARCHITECTS; SMBW

VISITING JUDGES

DEBORAH SAUNT
ARCHITECT, DSDHA
CHAIR OF THE RIBA AWARDS GROUP

PETER CLEGG
ARCHITECT, FEILDEN CLEGG BRADLEY STUDIOS

TONY CHAPMAN
RIBA HEAD OF AWARDS

FULL JURY

VISITING JUDGES, PLUS:

ANGELA BRADY
RIBA PRESIDENT

JIM EYRE
ARCHITECT, WILKINSON EYRE ARCHITECTS

THE MET
BANGKOK, THAILAND

WOHA WITH TANDEM ARCHITECTS 2001

CLIENT: PEBBLE BAY THAILAND
STRUCTURAL ENGINEER: WORLEY
SERVICES ENGINEER: EEC LINCOLNE SCOTT THAILAND
LANDSCAPE CONSULTANT: CICADA
CONTRACTOR: BOUYGUES THAI
CONTRACT VALUE: $132,000,000
DATE OF COMPLETION: DECEMBER 2009
GROSS INTERNAL AREA: 113,000 SQ. M
IMAGES: PATRICK BINGHAM-HALL (P. 45; BOTTOM; OPPOSITE; P. 49; P. 50;
    P. 51); TIM GRIFFITH – ARCAID (TOP; P. 48)

WOHA is a firm of young(ish) Singaporean architects who have
been transforming architectural thinking in South-East Asia with
a series of houses, apartment buildings, hotels, schools and train
stations. The Met residential tower block won an RIBA International
Award in 2010; it was also shortlisted for the RIBA Lubetkin
Prize that year, but was withdrawn owing to the political situation
in Thailand at the time. The sixty-six-storey perforated tower uses
the power of nature to cool the apartments: by punching holes
through the building and leaving vertical voids in the structure,
the architect has been able to introduce natural ventilation to flats
at all levels. The design funnels and enhances the power of the
breezes, and the staggered arrangement of the blocks allows
cross-ventilation. In addition, green creeper screens create living
walls all the way up the building to help shade the occupants and
further cool the building through the plants' transpiration. The

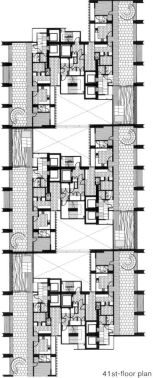

41st-floor plan

gaps in the structure are bridged by 'sky gardens', a series of interlocking external spaces that provide entertaining areas just off the living spaces. Apartments are accessed directly by lift, avoiding arguments about single- or double-loaded corridors. Residents also enjoy improved security, less noise and dust, and great views.

The building's strength derives from the fact that, like a lighthouse, it is wider at the bottom than at the top. It is tied together by U-shaped braces every six floors. Some of these floors are kept open and provide communal spaces: gardens, a gym and other leisure facilities, barbecue and seating areas. On top of the nine-storey podium building is a 50-metre swimming pool. Such generous provision in an apartment building would generally be confined to an underground space; here swimming is an act of urbanism.

It takes clever architecture to pull this off, and WOHA has proved itself to be a very intelligent practice. The Met shows that an alternative to the sleek, air-conditioned box can work in the tropics, and this has implications everywhere. This young, small but fast-growing practice has already won many international awards for its innovative architecture, including the 2007 Aga Khan Award for a housing development in Singapore, the Singapore President's Design Award in 2009 for the Genexis Theatre and in 2010 for the Stadium underground station; four RIBA International Awards (in 2010 for Singapore's Bras Basah underground station; in 2011 for The Met; Alila Villas Uluwatu in Bali, see p. 69; and Singapore's School of the Arts, see p. 75); and awards in Australia and the United States, and at the French MIPIM and the World Architecture Festival.

There is really no such thing as a typical WOHA building. Having already created low- and high-rise residential buildings, theatres, transport infrastructure, mixed-use commercial buildings, galleries and churches, and done new-build and conservation projects, the practice has touched most of the boundaries of the profession and in so doing has begun to shape a new architecture. WOHA approaches each new project by taking the client's brief and offering it up to the context. This meticulous research is vital, and for the architect it is one of the most enjoyable parts of the whole process. It always results in a series of sustainable options to agree with the client. Nor does the firm eschew the random; rather, it examines possibilities thrown up by the site, its context and its history, to see if it can add to the richness of the composition.

As urbanists as well as architects, the founding partners, Wong Mun Summ and Richard Hassell, understand that buildings make their own space but are also defined by what has gone before. With the Met they have produced for other architects what might be a template for high-rise sustainable living in a hot climate but which, for them, will be merely a jumping-off point for further explorations of the form and the building type. WOHA's work is important; just as after Mies, Seifert and Foster no architect could approach high-rise without taking their work in account, so WOHA's thinking and practice have redefined architecture in the early twenty-first century.

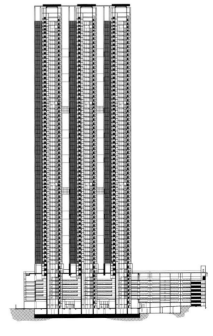

Section

GUANGZHOU OPERA HOUSE
GUANGZHOU, GUANGDONG, CHINA

ZAHA HADID ARCHITECTS

CLIENT: GUANGZHOU MUNICIPAL GOVERNMENT
STRUCTURAL ENGINEERS/CONTRACTORS: SHTK; GUANGZHOU PEARL RIVER
    FOREIGN INVESTMENT ARCHITECTURAL DESIGNING INSTITUTE
SERVICES ENGINEERS: GUANGZHOU PEARL RIVER FOREIGN INVESTMENT
    ARCHITECTURAL DESIGNING INSTITUTE; MAX FORDHAM; THE OK
    DESIGN GROUP
CONTRACT VALUE: CONFIDENTIAL
DATE OF COMPLETION: FEBRUARY 2010
GROSS INTERNAL AREA: 70,000 SQ. M
IMAGES: IWAN BAAN (TOP; P. 54 TOP; P. 55 TOP); VIRGILE SIMON BERTRAND
    (OPPOSITE; P. 54 BOTTOM); CHRISTIAN RICHTERS – VIEW (P. 55 BOTTOM)

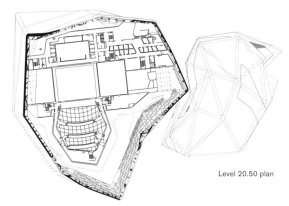

Level 20.50 plan

Welsh curmudgeons brought about a rude awakening to Zaha
Hadid's dream in 1994 of adding a touch of performing-arts
magic to Cardiff Bay, but with the Guangzhou Opera House
Britain's loss is finally China's gain. Of course, Hadid has moved
on since then and this is a very different environment, but there is
no doubt that practice has made perfect; this is surely a better
building than Cardiff was ever going to be.

   Hadid's characteristic shape-making does not always lead
to intimate interiors, but here – as we began to see in her MAXXI
modern art museum in Rome, winner of the RIBA Stirling Prize in
2010 – is a building that is as much about its internal places as it
is about external forms. Stairs sweep, walkways hover, the whole
thing is organized as a working piece of sculpture. At present
the Chinese belief that an opera house or theatre is a place for
witnessing a piece of theatre, and not one for hanging out with
cappuccinos or cocktails, means that these spaces are used only

during performances, but doubtless that will change, as so much else is changing in China. A smaller house, clad in white instead of the grey granite used for the rest of the scheme, provides a small performance space and is available for private hire.

Inside and out are linked by artfully placed windows that capture views of the city. Guangzhou is an avowedly industrial and commercial port city. As has been the case in Liverpool, it turned its back on its river because of a decline in trade but is now remaking the connection, here by means of a grand pedestrian boulevard with a six-lane road buried underneath. Where the boulevard meets the river, on an artificial mound that accommodates an undercroft, is the opera house. It contains a public entrance, a booking office, cafes and shops (you can buy a grand piano here if you are so inspired by a performance). It is a suitably theatrical space and a destination in its own right, where Hadid's Phaeno Science Centre in Wolfsburg, Germany, was only a thoroughfare and therefore less successful.

For all the auditorium's asymmetry, the acoustics are perfect. The auditorium has all the grandiosity and sumptuousness of Milan's La Scala or London's Royal Opera House, with gold-painted plasterwork beautifully and effectively treated, and sweeping balconies. Hadid has made a stage that befits her at last.

MASDAR INSTITUTE OF SCIENCE AND TECHNOLOGY

MASDAR CITY, ABU DHABI, UNITED ARAB EMIRATES

FOSTER + PARTNERS

CLIENT: MUBADALA DEVELOPMENT COMPANY
STRUCTURAL ENGINEER: ADAMS KARA TAYLOR
SERVICES ENGINEER: PHA CONSULT
CONTRACTOR: AL AHMADIAH HIP HING JV
CONTRACT VALUE: CONFIDENTIAL
DATE OF COMPLETION: OCTOBER 2010
GROSS INTERNAL AREA: 45,000 SQ. M
IMAGES: ROLAND HALBE (TOP); NIGEL YOUNG – FOSTER + PARTNERS
    (BOTTOM; OPPOSITE; P. 58; P. 59)

New architecture in the United Arab Emirates is not exactly
renowned for its sensitivity to either context or the environment.
But Foster's Masdar Institute is the first part of a masterplan for
a new quarter of Abu Dhabi, Masdar City, and is powered largely
by the sun – a plentiful local resource. What is more, these six
buildings, which include laboratories, teaching rooms and student
apartments, also respect the vernacular without being subservient
to it. The accommodation is shaded by perforated screens of
glass-reinforced concrete (GRC) that are reminiscent of traditional
Islamic architecture; the labs are clad in insulating cushions of
ETFE, which also reflect light down into the courtyards and the
narrow streets. These, in turn, were designed to provide much-
needed shade in a country where temperatures can reach 50°C.
These are real streets and real places. Thermal imaging was used
to identify hot spots on façades and measure the air temperatures
between buildings. The design responds directly to these findings.

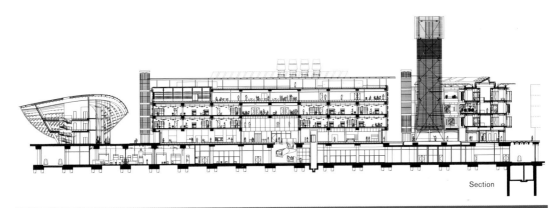

Section

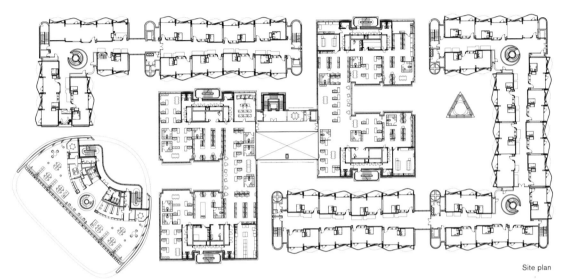

Site plan

Meanwhile, underneath the buildings – actually at ground-floor level, although it feels more like a basement – science fiction takes over from science fact: little four-person driverless people-movers scuttle about, avoiding one another and a forest of columns with the aid of computers. Appropriately, the institute shows a good degree of trust in technology.

A clever glulam roof to the Knowledge Centre allows in filtered light and natural ventilation, and provides a platform for the photovoltaics atop its spiky skin. All the buildings are orientated so as to minimize solar gain and reduce the energy required to cool them. Rooftop photovoltaics account for 30 per cent of Masdar's energy needs, and more electricity is produced through a fully functioning solar park that generates 10 megawatts of power. Shade-giving trees, such as jacaranda, and pools and channels of water are used to cool air temperatures, especially in the main courtyard, the Oasis. A 45-metre-tall wind tower symbolizes Masdar's aim of harnessing nature to the long-term benefit of the planet and is also a practical scientific tool for further research. This prototype complex is as sophisticated as ever a finished article could be.

MUSEUM OF FINE ARTS, BOSTON
BOSTON, MASSACHUSETTS, UNITED STATES

FOSTER + PARTNERS

CLIENT: MUSEUM OF FINE ARTS, BOSTON
STRUCTURAL ENGINEERS: BURO HAPPOLD; WEIDLINGER ASSOCIATES
SERVICES ENGINEERS: BURO HAPPOLD; WSP FLACK + KURTZ
CONTRACTOR: JOHN MORIARTY & ASSOCIATES
CONTRACT VALUE: $180,000,000
DATE OF COMPLETION: NOVEMBER 2010
GROSS INTERNAL AREA: 11,270 SQ. M
IMAGES: MUSEUM OF FINE ARTS, BOSTON (P. 63 TOP); NIGEL YOUNG –
    FOSTER + PARTNERS (BOTTOM; OPPOSITE; P. 62; P. 63 BOTTOM)

Norman Foster has re-orchestrated one of the world's finest
galleries, sampling some of his greatest hits – the Berlin
Reichstag (1999) and the Great Court of the British Museum,
London (2000) – to reinstate Guy Lowell's Beaux Arts plan, while
at the same time introducing light and clarity. The created space
houses the Art of the Americas Wing, with no fewer than fifty-
three new galleries arranged over four storeys. All this sits
against the backdrop of the work of no bit-part player I.M. Pei,
whose previous extension Foster + Partners has also restored
along with Lowell's original.

In fact here Pei (or rather his client) was the problem: with
his introduction of a new entrance at the western end of the
building and the simultaneous closure of the north entrance, the
short north–south axis was replaced by a very long west–east
axis, and, Americans not being the world's greatest pedestrians,
the eastern end of the building died. Foster + Partners has put all

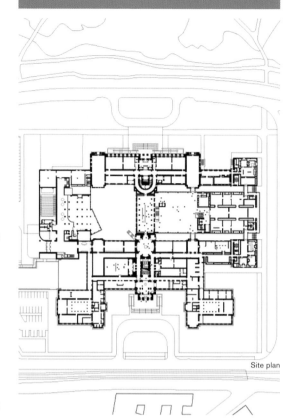

Site plan

that right, opening up the northern Fenway entrance and adding proper access, and reinstating the importance of the south door.

As in the case of the British Museum's Great Court, the architect has colonized a courtyard with a glass-covered cafe and a special exhibitions gallery incorporating state-of-the-art climate control. A smaller second courtyard remains an outside space and a reminder of the way things were; it is little used for much of the year and will eventually be glazed in when the masterplan is fully delivered. The central court helps visitors to orientate themselves and gives direct access to all the galleries, but does it in a non-dictatorial way. Routes are clear yet full of interest; in some places they take in views of the narrow slots between the old stone and new glass façades, spaces that are colonized by plants and art; in others they hug the new curtain walling that affords city views; occasionally they give on to little break-out spaces where visitors can rest or watch videos that fill in the background to the exhibitions or take them backstage. This is consummate architecture.

Section

VIRGINIA MUSEUM OF FINE ARTS
RICHMOND, VIRGINIA, UNITED STATES

RICK MATHER ARCHITECTS; SMBW

EXECUTIVE ARCHITECT: HANBURY EVANS WRIGHT VLATTAS + COMPANY
CLIENT: VIRGINIA MUSEUM OF FINE ARTS
CONTRACT VALUE: $150,000,000
DATE OF COMPLETION: APRIL 2010
GROSS INTERNAL AREA: 15,330 SQ. M (NEW BUILD); 3900 SQ. M (RENOVATION)
IMAGES: BILYANA DIMITROVA PHOTOGRAPHY (OPPOSITE, TOP); TRAVIS
    FULLERTON (BOTTOM); ANSEL OLSON (OPPOSITE, BOTTOM; P. 66; P. 67)

London-based Rick Mather has returned to his homeland to add a new wing to the Virginia Museum of Fine Arts. This is Mather at his best: making sense of what is there but adding his own finely honed stamp. The museum, which used to turn its back on the city with its blind façades, now addresses the grand boulevard on which it is sited in a very civic manner with a 12-metre-tall window of low-energy glass. The glazing deals with the lack of views out of the galleries, but it also breaks up and humanizes the façade. The spirits of both gallery visitors and citizens going about their daily business are lifted by the new architecture. Materially, the new building takes its cue from the old in its use of limestone. The project not only provides three new floors of gallery space, but also adds a shop, a library, a lecture hall, conservation studios, offices and a cafe and restaurant overlooking a sculpture garden.

With two existing, loosely connected buildings on the site, one dating from 1935 and the other from 1985, plus a number of

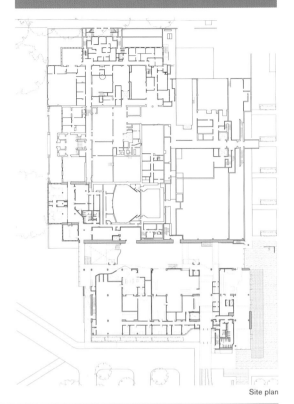

Site plan

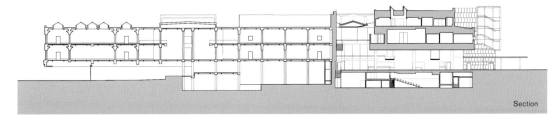

Section

other ad hoc additions, circulation was always difficult. Mather has made the layout seem natural with a series of sculptural stairs, walkways and lifts. As in his work at Oxford's Ashmolean Museum of Art and Archaeology (shortlisted for the RIBA Stirling Prize in 2010), these utilitarian objects have been turned into exhibits: a cantilevered stair clings caterpillar-like to a white wall, and a bridge, so slender in its steel profile, appears to float above the atrium. This misshapen cruciform space, dramatic and top-lit, unifies the three buildings that now make up the museum, and ensures that the galleries flow seamlessly into one another.

The landscaping stems from Mather's thinking, although it was carried out by other hands. The carefully managed landscape setting links a number of historic buildings that provide a perfect foil for Mather's modernism.

A generous mix of public and private funding allowed for the realization of the scheme. This is masterful museum-making, and a major contribution to the urban realm of Richmond.

THE RIBA
INTERNATIONAL AWARDS

ALILA VILLAS ULUWATU
BALI, INDONESIA

WOHA

CLIENT: BUKIT ULUWATU VILLA
STRUCTURAL/CIVIL ENGINEERS: WORLEY PARSONS; ATELIER ENAM
    STRUKTUR
MECHANICAL/ELECTRICAL ENGINEER: MAKESTHI ENGGAL ENGINEERING
CONTRACT VALUE: $100,000,000
DATE OF COMPLETION: JUNE 2009
GROSS INTERNAL AREA: 26,595 SQ. M
IMAGES: PATRICK BINGHAM-HALL (TOP); TIM GRIFFITH – ARCAID (CENTRE;
    BOTTOM)

Located in the dry savannah landscape of Bukit Peninsula on Bali's southern tip, this ecologically sustainable development of a fifty-suite hotel and thirty-five villas is Green Globe 21-rated.

Materials are locally sourced: for the wood, only recycled ulin (Borneo ironwood) and bamboo were used; the making of road cuttings provided the stone; and the fittings were made by local craftspeople. All this reduces the sense of conspicuous consumption that pervades most luxury resorts, and adds to the air of tranquillity. Rainwater and sewerage are recycled, heat pumps provide all the hot water, and the public areas are naturally ventilated. The gardens feature local plants that require far less water than non-native species, and support the native fauna. The project would exemplify truly sustainable tourism – if it weren't for those pesky aircraft required to get people there in the first place.

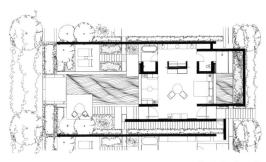

Hotel Villa floor plan

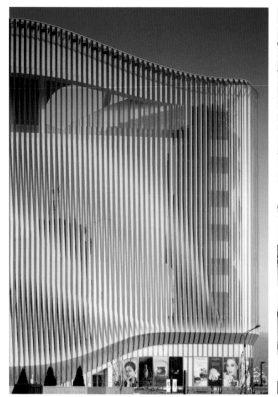

GALLERIA CENTERCITY

CHEONAN, SOUTH KOREA

UN STUDIO

CLIENT: HANWHA GALLERIA
FAÇADE CONSULTANT: KBM
CONTRACTOR: HANWHA E&C
CONTRACT VALUE: CONFIDENTIAL
DATE OF COMPLETION: DECEMBER 2010
GROSS INTERNAL AREA: 66,700 SQ. M
IMAGES: CHRISTIAN RICHTERS – VIEW

When in 2003 Future Systems gave us the silver disc-clad blue amoeba that is Selfridges in Birmingham, we thought the future of shopping had arrived. We had to wait a long time for UN Studio to come up with the next instalment, but the wait for this department store has been worthwhile.

The monochromatic reflective façade is a double skin; the external face is of laminated low-iron glass, while the internal face is of composite aluminium panels. The moire pattern of the curtain walling is created by the slender mullions that separate and support the two skins. The rounded floor plates and repeated curves unfold as shoppers move through the building. This intriguing project intelligently addresses the transience of our global shopping culture, and creates a unique and distinctive building type.

Section

IRON MARKET
PORT-AU-PRINCE, HAITI

JOHN MCASLAN + PARTNERS

CLIENT/PRINCIPAL COLLABORATOR: INSTITUT DE SAUVEGARDE DU
    PATRIMOINE NATIONAL ON BEHALF OF THE MUNICIPALITY OF
    PORT-AU-PRINCE
SPONSORS: CLINTON GLOBAL INITIATIVE; DIGICEL
STRUCTURAL ENGINEER: AXIS DESIGN GROUP
STEEL ENGINEER: O'BRIEN STEEL CONSULTING
HISTORIC ENGINEER: ALAN BAXTER & ASSOCIATES
CONTRACTOR: GDG BÉTON ET CONSTRUCTION
CONTRACT VALUE: CONFIDENTIAL
DATE OF COMPLETION: JANUARY 2011
GROSS INTERNAL AREA: 4645 SQ. M
IMAGES: HUFTON & CROW – VIEW (BOTTOM); JOHN MCASLAN + PARTNERS
    (CENTRE); ALLISON SHELLEY (TOP)

When the Haiti earthquake of 2010 mangled Port-au-Prince's late nineteenth-century Iron Market, it destroyed one of the country's landmarks. It was built in France and originally destined for Cairo to serve as a railway station, but the vagaries of history, tides or captains led it to end up in Haiti, where it served as a market hall until it was ravaged first by fire in 2008 and then by earthquake.

    Working on a pro-bono basis, the architect led an international multidisciplinary team, collaborating with local craftsmen, to salvage what they could of the original twisted structure and other materials, and painstakingly reconstruct the rest. Funded by Irish telecoms billionaire Denis O'Brien, the Iron Market is now fully functioning, with 700 stallholders, and forms the cornerstone of a new cultural hub for the city.

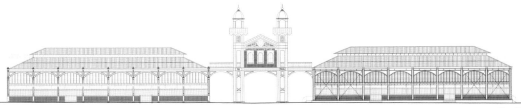

Elevation

LABORATORY BUILDING

BASEL, SWITZERLAND

DAVID CHIPPERFIELD ARCHITECTS

CLIENT: NOVARTIS
STRUCTURAL ENGINEER: WALT + GALMARINI
SERVICES ENGINEERS: GB CONSULT; FACT
CONTRACTORS: IMPLENIA; DRESSLER BAU
CONTRACT VALUE: CONFIDENTIAL
DATE OF COMPLETION: MAY 2010
GROSS INTERNAL AREA: 11,600 SQ. M
IMAGES: ULRICH SCHWARZ (TOP); UTE ZSCHARNT (BOTTOM)

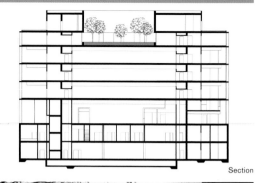

Section

The colonnade is a recurring theme in David Chipperfield's architecture, and it adds a classical seriousness to this 'laboratory of the future' for the Novartis pharmaceutical company; it also picks up on the use of the device in neighbouring buildings. The load-bearing, multi-angular, pre-cast concrete columns extend to all the building's façades and structure. Inside, 27-metre-long beams create column-free spaces for flexible working arrangements. Services are also neatly incorporated into these beams. There is poetry in the simplicity of this arrangement, and it is enhanced by a three-storey yellow sculptural staircase from Ross Lovegrove, as well as by an installation by Serge Spritzer in the enclosed garden on the top floor.

LOFT GARDENS
ISTANBUL, TURKEY

TABANLIOGLU ARCHITECTS

CLIENTS: AKFEN GAYRIMENKUL; SAGLAM CONSTRUCTION
CONTRACTOR: AKFEN INSAAT TURIZM VE TICARET
CONTRACT VALUE: £12,400,00
DATE OF COMPLETION: 2010
GROSS INTERNAL AREA: 22,500 SQ. M
IMAGES: HÉLÈNE BINET

This twenty-one-storey residential building takes the Miesian tower model and updates and humanizes it subtly by manipulating its pure shape into an articulated inhabited form. High-rise garden patios are inserted into the façade as a counterpoint to the protruding bay windows, and deepen the play of solid and void within the façade. Plan and section are organized to create a range of apartment types of great spatial variety; some are horizontal, based around patios, others are vertical around double-height spaces. Inside, the designers display an unabashed passion for the aesthetic of the industrial loft, with exposed services and structure and the use of concrete, steel and timber. The Loft Gardens are an extreme demonstration of elegance and restraint within a subtly modified typology.

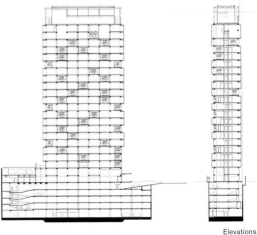

Elevations

NORTH COLLEGE, RICE UNIVERSITY

HOUSTON, TEXAS, UNITED STATES

HOPKINS ARCHITECTS

CLIENT: BARBARA WHITE BRYSON
STRUCTURAL ENGINEERS: HAYNES WALEY ASSOCIATES; ULRICH ENGINEERS
CONTRACTOR: LINBECK GROUP
CONTRACT VALUE: $110,000,000
DATE OF COMPLETION: AUGUST 2009
GROSS INTERNAL AREA: 300,000 SQ. M
IMAGES: ROBERT BENSON

Site plan

On a campus established in 1912 and that features a collection of additions by such architects as César Pelli, Ricardo Bofill and James Stirling and Michael Wilford, Hopkins Architects was commissioned to design two new residential colleges. Between them, the new McMurtry and Duncan colleges provide some 400 rooms, housing up to 650 students. Each quadrangle is completed by a 'commons', or dining space, the communal heart of the colleges.

The self-supporting walls are built with an 8-inch-deep (20.3 cm) brick. Their red colour reflects the rich character of the existing campus buildings. The use of a mortar with a high lime content produces a flexibility that avoids the need for expansion joints. This material honesty took the Texas construction industry by surprise and required extensive dialogue between architect, client, engineers and contractor.

SCHOOL OF THE ARTS
SINGAPORE

WOHA

CLIENT: MINISTRY OF INFORMATION, COMMUNICATION AND THE ARTS
STRUCTURAL/CIVIL ENGINEER: WORLEY PARSONS
MECHANICAL/ELECTRICAL ENGINEER: WSP LINCOLNE SCOTT
CONTRACTOR: TIONG AIK CONSTRUCTION
CONTRACT VALUE: $100,000,000
DATE OF COMPLETION: 2010
GROSS INTERNAL AREA: 52,945 SQ. M
IMAGES: PATRICK BINGHAM-HALL

The aim of this new arts-based school for thirteen- to eighteen-year-olds is 'to groom the next generation of artists, creative professionals and individuals who are passionate for and committed to the arts in a multicultural society'. It is a tall order, to which the architect has responded splendidly.

This pair of vegetation-clad slab blocks, which guards an open atrium criss-crossed by walkways, represents an exploration of ideas for high-density educational spaces in the urban tropics. On a compact inner-city site, the buildings allow a seamless integration of indoor and outdoor spaces for education, interaction, communication and exhibition. The podium contains a theatre, a concert hall and a number of informal performance spaces. It provides a beautiful, safe and secure environment for arts education.

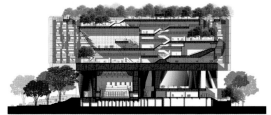

Section

STANISLAVSKY FACTORY
MOSCOW, RUSSIA

JOHN MCASLAN + PARTNERS

EXECUTIVE ARCHITECT: ADM MOSCOW
CLIENT: SERGEY GORDEEV
STRUCTURAL ENGINEER: ARUP
CONTRACTOR: MEBE CONSTRUCTION
CONTRACT VALUE: CONFIDENTIAL
DATE OF COMPLETION: JANUARY 2011
GROSS INTERNAL AREA: 60,400 SQ. M
IMAGE: JOHN MCASLAN + PARTNERS

Post-Soviet Moscow doesn't do old, so it was something of a first for McAslan to take a whole quarter, hard by Red Square, and regenerate a series of buildings, interlacing them with fine new work to produce a mixed-use scheme. Old factories and classically proportioned houses, the early twentieth-century building that was home to actor and theatre director Konstantin Stanislavsky and the Moscow Art Theatre: all have been lovingly repaired, reworked and reused. The theatre is now an arts centre; the rest are offices, flats, restaurants and a hotel. All this sits happily within a masterplan, also by McAslan, that provides a gently restrained setting for the buildings new and old. An important little corner of Moscow has been saved.

Site plan

Section

YOUTH MENTAL HEALTH BUILDING
UNIVERSITY OF SYDNEY, AUSTRALIA

BVN

CLIENT: UNIVERSITY OF SYDNEY
CONTRACTOR: BUILDCORP
CONTRACT VALUE: $14,000,000
DATE OF COMPLETION: AUGUST 2009
GROSS INTERNAL AREA: 3000 SQ. M
IMAGES: JOHN GOLLINGS – ARCAID

This building has a heritage-listed façade and a tough context, situated as it is in the former rag-trade area of Sydney. In a demonstration of intelligent and highly appropriate architecture, BVN has responded with a delightful mongrel of a building, balancing a glass box containing the laboratories on top of the retained two-storey structure. The resulting composition is visually exciting and a major addition to the streetscape.

Materially, the use of recycled timber and steel reflects the gritty urban context, while the translucent glass panels give the building modernity and produce an excellent light-filled working environment. In the atrium and staircase, which link all the areas, the same materials are just as tactile and just as tough.

THE RIBA MANSER MEDAL
IN ASSOCIATION WITH HSBC PRIVATE BANK

The objectives of the RIBA Manser Medal are to encourage innovation in house design, to show how social and technological ambitions can be met by intelligent design, and to produce exemplars to be taken up by the wider house-building industry. The prize is named after Michael Manser, former RIBA President, who is well known for his own steel-and-glass house designs.

Michael Manser had for a number of years chaired the National Homebuilder Design Awards, which were run by Mike Gazzard. RIBA Honorary Fellow Gazzard approached Tony Chapman, custodian of all the RIBA's awards, about how to mark Manser's contribution. It was agreed to create an award in his name for one-off houses, by way of balancing the Housing Design Awards, which are exclusively for housing schemes. The Manser Medal was presented as part of the National Homebuilder Design Awards for two years, before switching stables in 2003 to become part of the RIBA Awards. In 2006 the National Homebuilder Design Awards were bought by EMAP, long-term sponsors of the RIBA's awards programme. The award has since been presented at the RIBA Awards Dinner, at the RIBA Stirling Prize Dinner and latterly at its own ceremony.

The RIBA Manser Medal was relaunched in 2010 with HSBC Private Bank as the exclusive sponsor. Eligibility for the medal reverted to the traditional position of being open only to one-off houses. The prize money was doubled to £10,000, and a new trophy was commissioned from artist Petr Weigl, who also designed the RIBA Lubetkin Prize. All the RIBA Award-winning houses in the United Kingdom were considered for this year's medal, and six were shortlisted. The winner was announced at the RIBA in November 2011.

For previous winners of the medal, see p. 245.

WINNER

HAMPSTEAD LANE
LONDON N6
DUGGAN MORRIS ARCHITECTS

SHORTLIST

THE BALANCING BARN
THORINGTON, SUFFOLK
MVRDV WITH MOLE ARCHITECTS

HOUSE IN EPSOM
THE RIDGE, EPSOM
ELDRIDGE SMERIN

MISSION HALL
RICKMAN'S LANE, PLAISTOW,
WEST SUSSEX
ADAM RICHARDS ARCHITECTS

TY HEDFAN
PONTFAEN, BRECON, POWYS
FEATHERSTONE YOUNG

WATSON HOUSE
NEW FOREST NATIONAL PARK
JOHN PARDEY ARCHITECTS

JUDGES

MICHAEL MANSER, CBE
FORMER RIBA PRESIDENT

FRIEDRICH LUDEWIG
ARCHITECT, ACME

JO VAN HEYNINGEN
ARCHITECT, VAN HEYNINGEN AND
HAWARD ARCHITECTS

PETER MACKIE
PROPERTY VISION, A DIVISION OF
HSBC PRIVATE BANK

TONY CHAPMAN
RIBA HEAD OF AWARDS

HAMPSTEAD LANE
LONDON N6

DUGGAN MORRIS ARCHITECTS

CLIENT: PRIVATE
STRUCTURAL ENGINEER: ELLIOTT WOOD PARTNERSHIP
CONTRACTOR: ME CONSTRUCTION
CONTRACT VALUE: £500,000
DATE OF COMPLETION: FEBRUARY 2010
GROSS INTERNAL AREA: 200 SQ. M
IMAGES: JAMES BRITTAIN – VIEW

Love them or hate them, brutalist buildings of the 1960s
and 1970s all too often suffer unsympathetic renovation or
replacement, the latter being the likely fate of this tough blockwork house before enlightened clients rescued it.

Although seemingly indestructible, concrete needs tender
loving care every bit as much as timber and glass. This sensitive
and rigorous renovation has taken the austere, self-built structure,
which presents itself unpromisingly to the street and was internally
compromised by a maze of cellular rooms, and made it into a
delightful house that lifts the spirits.

Key to the project's success is the removal of two internal
walls that ran the depth of the house; these have been replaced by
a straightforward steel structure. This is perhaps the obvious move,
but it is a question of how you do it. The main room is flooded with
natural light, while the intimacy of the bedrooms has been retained.
Two of these open out on to the garden, as does the main living–
eating–cooking space, while the mezzanine master bedroom
overlooks it across a strip of planted roof. The garden is a delight –
a rectangle of almost Scandinavian landscape that in summer
doubles the living space thanks to the glazed sliding doors.

Despite the extensive renovation, the character and the
qualities of the original brutalist structure remain intact, taking on

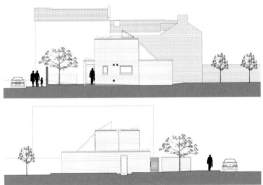

Elevations

an altogether different quality when set against the sensitive interventions that define this project. This has largely been achieved by an apparently judicious assessment of which elements should be kept in place – such as the timber staircase with its diagonal balustrading – in order to preserve the integrity of the original house.

The project has been a labour of love, approached with an appreciation of and care for the house and its history. The clients, considerable architects in their own right, have taken the sensible but unusual and modest step of calling in other architects to realize their dream. The result is a joy to step into. As Michael Manser said in his summation, this is truly a house of its time and of the moment.

THE BALANCING BARN
THORINGTON, SUFFOLK

MVRDV WITH MOLE ARCHITECTS

CLIENT: LIVING ARCHITECTURE

In one sense, it is not difficult to do something dramatic in the flat hinterland of the Suffolk coast, but what the two sets of architects have achieved is truly unique. There is more of a tradition of radical single-minded projects in MVRDV's homeland of The Netherlands than there is in Britain, and it takes a brave client to allow the practice to translate such ideas to East Anglia.

This, then, is a Dutch barn for a very English landscape, or, more accurately perhaps, a stretched Airstream caravan about to topple over the edge.

For the full citation, see p. 138.

HOUSE IN EPSOM
THE RIDGE, EPSOM

ELDRIDGE SMERIN

CLIENTS: IAN AND LELYANA HARRIS

The house is made up of two wings, one the home, the other the swimming pool, while a sculptured landscape garden makes a rhomboid of the whole plan. The building sits slightly submerged in its golf-course setting; the lower-floor study and bedrooms and the indoor pool open on to a sunken landscape and feel secluded yet secure.

The project is in a long architectural tradition of the large and lavish private house, one that promotes experimentation with the building type, turning it into an art form.

For the full citation, see p. 157.

MISSION HALL
RICKMAN'S LANE, PLAISTOW, WEST SUSSEX

ADAM RICHARDS ARCHITECTS

CLIENTS: NICHOLAS TAYLOR AND DEAN WHEELER

This delightful house retains the memory of the chapel that occupied the site until it was undermined by the roots of an ancient oak. The oak remains, its branches all but cradling the upper room of one of the two slim offset buildings, one of which in its apsidal form evokes the chapel and faces the road; the other, more of a pavilion, looks out over the elaborate Sussex countryside. This is architecture that is as bespoke as the walnut furniture that shapes the house's rich interiors.

For the full citation, see p. 158.

TY HEDFAN
PONTFAEN, BRECON, POWYS

FEATHERSTONE YOUNG

CLIENTS: JEREMY YOUNG AND SARAH FEATHERSTONE

Built on a tight, sloping riverside plot with a cantilever that circumvents the 7-metre no-build zone adjacent to the river, this contemporary building not only feels at one with the landscape but also, in the use of materials and by clever consideration of the orientation of the house, blends into the architecture of the nearby village. This confident and innovative solution to the demands of a difficult site has provided the architect-owners with a delightful rural retreat.

For the full citation, see p. 129.

WATSON HOUSE
NEW FOREST NATIONAL PARK

JOHN PARDEY ARCHITECTS

CLIENTS: CHARLES AND FIONA WATSON

There is an integrity and an elegant simplicity to this house, a single long, linear shape in a New Forest clearing. It is a strong idea, but is not overcooked.

The timber panels allowed the building to be constructed quickly. The large areas of glass are recessed under overhangs in order to minimize heat gain and strengthen the inside–outside flow of space. Tiny windows at skirting level are perfect for pets to look out of. This is a poetic building of a type that is seldom seen in the English environment.

For the full citation, see p. 155.

THE STEPHEN LAWRENCE PRIZE
SUPPORTED BY THE MARCO GOLDSCHMIED FOUNDATION

The Stephen Lawrence Prize is supported by
the Marco Goldschmied Foundation. The prize
commemorates the teenager who was just
setting out on the road to becoming an architect
when he was murdered in 1993. It rewards the
best examples of projects with a construction
budget of less than £1,000,000. In addition to
the £5000 prize money, Marco Goldschmied
donates £10,000 to fund the Stephen Lawrence
Scholarship at the Architectural Association
in London.

The Stephen Lawrence Prize was established
in 1998 to draw attention to the Stephen Lawrence
Trust, which assists young black students in
studying architecture, and to reward the creativity
required for smaller projects with low budgets.

For previous winners of the prize, see p. 245.

WINNER

**ST PATRICK'S CATHOLIC
PRIMARY SCHOOL LIBRARY
AND MUSIC ROOM**
HOLMES ROAD, LONDON NW5
COFFEY ARCHITECTS

SHORTLIST

BROWN'S DENTAL PRACTICE
FORE STREET, IVYBRIDGE
DAVID SHEPPARD ARCHITECTS

HOXTON HOUSE
BUTTESLAND STREET, LONDON N1
DAVID MIKHAIL ARCHITECTS

**MARSHLAND DISCOVERY ZONE,
RSPB RAINHAM MARSHES**
PURFLEET, ESSEX
PETER BEARD_LANDROOM

TY HEDFAN
PONTFAEN, BRECON, POWYS
FEATHERSTONE YOUNG

THE WHITE HOUSE
GRISHIPOL, ISLE OF COLL,
INNER HEBRIDES
WT ARCHITECTURE

JUDGES

MARCO GOLDSCHMIED
ARCHITECT

PHILIP GUMUCHDJIAN
ARCHITECT, GUMUCHDJIAN
ARCHITECTS

DOREEN LAWRENCE, OBE

ST PATRICK'S CATHOLIC PRIMARY SCHOOL LIBRARY AND MUSIC ROOM
HOLMES ROAD, LONDON NW5

COFFEY ARCHITECTS

CLIENT: ST PATRICK'S CATHOLIC PRIMARY SCHOOL
STRUCTURAL ENGINEER: RODRIGUES ASSOCIATES
SERVICES ENGINEER: CON-SERV
CONTRACTOR: BOLT & HEEKS
CONTRACT VALUE: £350,000
DATE OF COMPLETION: FEBRUARY 2011
GROSS INTERNAL AREA: 60 SQ. M
IMAGES: TIMOTHY SOAR

'Less is more' sums up this tiny yet delightful and ingenious school extension, which provides a library, a music room and a storeroom. The St Patrick's Catholic Primary School Library and Music Room is that rare achievement: a space that allows for a wide variety of uses, yet retains the intimate and personal atmosphere of a bespoke single-function design.

The design process took the client from the original notion of two separate 'rooms' on the roof of the existing 1960s building to a more usable ground-level single volume that was far less disruptive to construct. The effortless and elegant integration of structure, internal finishes and fixed furniture creates a place that generations of pupils will fondly remember in years to come.

The building has a simplicity that comes from a straightforward plan and the prevailing expression of just two materials: timber, clearly articulated in the interior of the space, and zinc sheets on the external skin. This clarity and truth to materials are all too often absent in buildings of this scale. Internally, the space is lined, at ground level, by bookshelves on three sides and, on the first-floor mezzanine, by stored musical instruments. The central volume created by this arrangement is open and flexible, allowing the area to be used for musical practice, performances and group reading – in fact, for whatever the school requires.

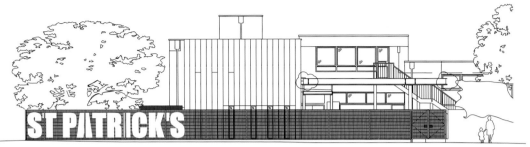

Elevation

However, this simple arrangement is given an extra dimension by the openable glass wall, which, with a freestanding external canopy, creates an informal proscenium for play. The deceptively uncomplicated external canopy links the new and the old, and provides a technical and visual language that can, as funds permit, be readily applied to enhance and revitalize other parts of the original building. The canopy also gracefully enhances the functionality of both the indoor and the outdoor spaces.

In each manifestation the elegantly designed and beautifully lit space displays astonishing integrity and generates delight. This project marks that rare occasion when a small budget in the hands of a thoughtful and ingenious architect lays the seed for the step-by-step transformation of an entire institution.

BROWN'S DENTAL PRACTICE
FORE STREET, IVYBRIDGE

DAVID SHEPPARD ARCHITECTS

CLIENTS: LORNA AND DEREK BROWN

The cleverness of this building lies in the tension between the sculptural response to the site's complex topography and what is essentially a very straightforward plan. The result is a building that appears to be intricate, offering visitors a sense of exploration and surprise, but is both legible and efficient. The cedar cladding has narrow glazed slots between the planks, a discreet device that is barely visible from the outside but gives people inside the treatment room glimpses of the outdoor world.

For the full citation, see p. 146.

HOXTON HOUSE
BUTTESLAND STREET, LONDON N1

DAVID MIKHAIL ARCHITECTS

CLIENT: PRIVATE

The architect's approach in realizing the full potential of this typical four-storey London terraced house, and in making sense of it, is surprisingly straightforward and simple. The thoughtful and intelligent response seems so obvious and successful that it is hard to imagine why it has not been done before. It is undoubtedly a solution that advances the notion of how we might continue to adapt traditional houses for the evolving needs of the future.

For the full citation, see p. 171.

MARSHLAND DISCOVERY ZONE, RSPB RAINHAM MARSHES
PURFLEET, ESSEX

PETER BEARD_LANDROOM

CLIENT: THE ROYAL SOCIETY FOR THE PROTECTION OF BIRDS

The estuarine landscape of Rainham Marshes is completely dominated by the horizontal. The marshes here have a wasteland feel that raises many questions as to how we can best use this type of landscape in a creative and productive way.

The same question arises regarding industrial objects, such as rusting sea containers: do we throw them away, or should we dismantle and reuse them in a new way? With the Marshland Discovery Zone, the architect has confronted this question head on, and the results have a strange beauty.

For the full citation, see p. 141.

TY HEDFAN
PONTFAEN, BRECON, POWYS

FEATHERSTONE YOUNG

CLIENTS: JEREMY YOUNG AND SARAH FEATHERSTONE

Built on a tight, sloping riverside plot with a cantilever that circumvents the 7-metre no-build zone adjacent to the river, this contemporary building not only feels at one with the landscape but also, in the use of materials and by clever consideration of the orientation of the house, blends into the architecture of the nearby village. This confident and innovative solution to the demands of a difficult site has provided the architect-owners with a delightful rural retreat.

For the full citation, see p. 129.

THE WHITE HOUSE
GRISHIPOL, ISLE OF COLL, INNER HEBRIDES

WT ARCHITECTURE

CLIENTS: ALEX AND SEONAID MACLEAN

The site, at the rocky edge of the Coll, is dramatic and exposed. The clients carefully selected an architect who shared their vision of building a new house incorporating an existing ruin, and have been rewarded by the imagination and sensitivity with which it has been done.

While the ruin has been consolidated, it retains the scars of age, with only half of it containing accommodation; the other half, including a great cleft stitched together by a steel 'window' frame, is kept as an open courtyard.

For the full citation, see p. 110.

THE RIBA CLIENT OF THE YEAR
SUPPORTED BY THE BLOXHAM CHARITABLE TRUST

The RIBA Client of the Year was established in 1998 to acknowledge the significant role played by the client in the creation of fine architecture. The RIBA's partner for many years was Arts Council England. Since 2010 the award has been supported by the Bloxham Charitable Trust.

In order to be considered for the award, it is necessary for the client to have commissioned an RIBA Award-winning building in the year in question. Traditionally, the award is presented to a client that has a track record of exemplary commissioning, rather than a client that has commissioned a one-off building. Occasionally, however, the RIBA rewards the successful culmination of a series of commissions that bring an institution up to date and make it work for a wider constituency than ever before.

For previous winners of the award, see p. 246.

WINNER

ROYAL SHAKESPEARE COMPANY

SHORTLIST

CHATHAM HISTORIC
   DOCKYARD TRUST
LAND SECURITIES
LONDON BOROUGH OF HACKNEY
THE ROYAL SOCIETY FOR
   THE PROTECTION OF BIRDS

JUDGES

DEBORAH SAUNT
ARCHITECT, DSDHA
CHAIR OF THE RIBA AWARDS GROUP

CINDY WALTERS
ARCHITECT, WALTERS AND COHEN

TONY CHAPMAN
RIBA HEAD OF AWARDS

ROYAL SHAKESPEARE COMPANY for the Royal Shakespeare and Swan Theatres, Stratford-upon-Avon, by Bennetts Associates.

The Royal Shakespeare Company has been an exceptional client, as shown not only by the transformation of the Royal Shakespeare and Swan Theatres and the creation of the Chapel Lane studios, all with Bennetts Associates, but also by Ian Ritchie's temporary Courtyard Theatre (which, together with the London Eye and the Eiffel Tower, ranks among the world's best temporary structures). The auditorium within Ritchie's Cor-ten shell acted as a working experiment that led to the intimacy and superb acoustics of the new Royal Shakespeare Theatre.

By means of a long, complex and exhaustive process, working through internal consultation at all levels and with a number of architects, the RSC has brought into the theatre people who would never have dreamed of going before, thereby giving them theatrical and architectural experiences to treasure for the rest of their lives. The experience has even been translated across the Atlantic, with a full-size temporary replica of the Royal Shakespeare Theatre's new auditorium appearing in New York City.

These projects represent a formidable portfolio of high-quality patronage, and have been carried out in a collaborative way, with the RSC's theatrical designers fully integrated with the architect-led teams. All this has led to a revitalized relationship between the RSC and the town of Stratford-upon-Avon.

For the full project citation, see pp. 36–39.

CHATHAM HISTORIC DOCKYARD TRUST for No. 1
Smithery, The Historic Dockyard, by Van Heyningen and Haward
Architects.

The trust is responsible for a highly complex and constrained
site, and has brought back into productive, viable use almost all
of its listed buildings. As well as attracting an ever-increasing
number of visitors, the Historic Dockyard is home to 400 people
and 140 businesses employing more than 1000 people.

The trust has high expectations of its architects and its slim
budgets, but its strong leadership ensures that the individual
contributions of its partners, consultants and contractors come
together to best effect.

For the full project citation, see p. 159.

LAND SECURITIES for One New Change by Ateliers Jean Nouvel with Sidell Gibson Architects, and New Street Square by Bennetts Associates, both in London.

With One New Change, Land Securities has commissioned from architects of international repute a piece of contemporary architecture that complements its neo-classical surroundings.

One New Change sets the standard for other commercial clients to follow in the future. Land Securities' 2009 RIBA Award-winning New Street Square, with Bennetts, showed how commercial developments can transform the public realm.

For the full project citation, see p. 176.

LONDON BOROUGH OF HACKNEY for Hackney Service Centre by Hopkins Architects, and Stoke Newington School and Sixth Form by Jestico + Whiles.

With Hopkins's Hackney Service Centre, the council set design and sustainability criteria that went beyond the minimum. It also set tough cost targets, but encouraged and supported the design team in looking at innovative ways to tackle issues. Working with Hackney was an exemplar of the co-design process. It adopts the same approach for all its new projects, and with Jestico + Whiles at Stoke Newington School it helped to repair, reinterpret and preserve a challenging existing building as well as extend it. The resulting buildings are a clear response to the council's original vision.

For the full project citations, see pp. 170 and 180.

THE ROYAL SOCIETY FOR THE PROTECTION OF BIRDS
for Marshland Discovery Zone, RSPB Rainham Marshes,
Purfleet, Essex, by Peter Beard_Landroom, and Reception Hide
Complex, Titchwell Marsh, Titchwell, Norfolk, by Haysom Ward
Miller Architects.

As an organization the RSPB has recognized the key role
architecture has to play in supporting its core programme of
conservation of wildlife and the natural world. In recent years
the RSPB has shown highly active support and promotion of
innovation in architecture through its commissioning of architects
for a range of projects. It has recognized that the involvement of
architects in even modest-scaled projects can have a big impact.

For the full project citations, see pp. 141 and 143.

THE RIBA AWARDS

The RIBA Awards were established in 1966. RIBA members are invited to enter projects for all the RIBA building awards in the first two months of the year. Entries are first visited by a local architect to see if they merit a visit from a full regional jury of three, consisting of an architect chair from outside the region, one from that region and a 'lay' juror, such as an engineer, client, artist or journalist. The chairs of the regional juries report to the Awards Group (the scheme's advisory panel), which has the right to query if a scheme not given an award was, in its view, worthy of one. In this case, the jury chair may, in consultation with the other members of his or her jury, agree to an award. The Awards Group has no right to overturn an award. These awards are presented in the RIBA regions.

JUDGES

THE REGIONAL JUDGES ARE LISTED IN THE FOLLOWING ORDER: CHAIR, REGIONAL REPRESENTATIVE AND LAY ASSESSOR

SCOTLAND

GEORGE FERGUSON
NEIL BAXTER/DAVID DUNBAR
DAPHNE THISSEN

NORTHERN IRELAND

SORAYA KHAN
CIARÁN MACKEL
EILEEN ADAMS

NORTH-EAST

NEIL MATHEWS
ERIC CARTER
TIM LUCAS

NORTH-WEST

SIMON ALLFORD
JONATHAN FALKINGHAM
CLIVE BIRCH

YORKSHIRE

ALAN PERT
IAN COLLINS
ROD HOLMES

WALES

JONATHAN SPEIRS
ANDREW SUTTON
MILICA KITSON

WEST MIDLANDS

SHAHRIAR NASSER
PETER BROWNHILL
RICHARD BRYANT

EAST MIDLANDS

MARY BOWMAN
JULIAN OWEN
MARTIN WILLEY

EAST

SIMON HUDSPITH
RICHARD TAVENER
ANDREW SCOONES

SOUTH-WEST

ADRIAN GALE
MARK PEARSON
ISABEL ALLEN

WESSEX

ADRIAN GALE
CATHERINE GANDON
ISABEL ALLEN

SOUTH

OLIVER RICHARDS
GRAHAM WHITEHOUSE
DORIS LOCKHART SAATCHI

SOUTH-EAST

ANDREW WAUGH
DAVID FALLA
ALAN BAXTER

LONDON EAST

KAY HUGHES
MATTHEW LLOYD
KATE GOODWIN

LONDON NORTH

NEIL GILLESPIE
ROBERT KENNETT
ALICE BLACK

LONDON SOUTH

KEITH BROWNLIE
STUART PIERCY
MOIRA GEMMILL

LONDON WEST

MICHAEL JONES
MARY DUGGAN
NICK MCKEOGH

EUROPEAN UNION

DEBORAH SAUNT (CHAIR)
BOB ALLIES
GIANNI BOTSFORD
ALISON BROOKS
TONY CHAPMAN
PETER CLEGG
TOM DYCKHOFF
PAUL FINCH
MURRAY FRASER
RICHARD GRIFFITHS
PHILIP GUMUCHDJIAN
BILL TAYLOR
CINDY WALTERS

THE HOUL
CASTLE DOUGLAS, DUMFRIES & GALLOWAY

SIMON WINSTANLEY ARCHITECTS

CLIENT: SIMON WINSTANLEY
STRUCTURAL ENGINEER: ASHER ASSOCIATES
SERVICES ENGINEER: PATERSON LANDSCAPE
CONTRACTOR: 36 CONSTRUCTION
CONTRACT VALUE: £306,000
DATE OF COMPLETION: DECEMBER 2009
GROSS INTERNAL AREA: 185 SQ. M
IMAGES: ANDREW LEE

This elegant timber-clad, single-storey 'long house' is set into a hillside, commanding views over the valley of the River Ken to the Rhinns of Kells. The principal accommodation is in a steel-framed structure below a standing-seam zinc roof, which is cantilevered on all sides to create additional shelter, and which follows the line of the hillside, reducing the visual impact of the building. Walls are of highly insulated timber-framed panels clad in cedar weatherboarding. The house achieves a zero carbon rating through its high levels of insulation, its heat-recovery ventilation, its air-source heat pump and its wind turbine. As a home, the building, which is immaculately detailed, feels particularly light and spacious.

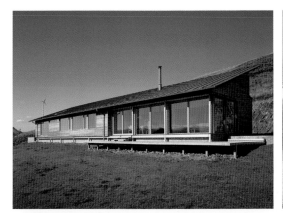

LINBURN CENTRE FOR SCOTTISH WAR BLINDED

LINBURN WILKIESTON, KIRKNEWTON, EDINBURGH

PAGE\PARK

CLIENT: ROYAL BLIND
STRUCTURAL ENGINEER: SKM ANTHONY HUNT (EDINBURGH)
SERVICES ENGINEER: HARLEY HADDOW
CONTRACTOR: W.H. BROWN CONSTRUCTION
CONTRACT VALUE: £2,647,031
DATE OF COMPLETION: JANUARY 2011
GROSS INTERNAL AREA: 791 SQ. M
IMAGES: ANDREW LEE (TOP; BOTTOM); PAGE\PARK (CENTRE)

This elegant building, sitting beautifully in its West Lothian landscape, demonstrates the benefits of enlightened architectural patronage by a distinguished charitable trust. Despite, oddly, taking its inspiration from a hand-carved Chinese celestial dragon, the building's sinuous plan form makes it legible for its users, all of whom suffer some level of visual impairment. The sweeping zinc-covered roof and limited palette of external materials generate a sophisticated building, free of institutional connotations. Rooms are accessed from a single broad circulation spine, which connects the social, work and rehabilitation spaces; access to each is subtly differentiated by variations in the internal colour palette.

THE MCMANUS
ALBERT SQUARE, DUNDEE

PAGE\PARK

CLIENT/STRUCTURAL ENGINEER: DUNDEE CITY COUNCIL
CONTRACTOR: MUIRFIELD CONTRACTS
CONTRACT VALUE: £9,500,000
DATE OF COMPLETION: NOVEMBER 2009
GROSS INTERNAL AREA: 4720 SQ. M
IMAGES: ANDREW LEE

This important new cultural facility for Dundee adapts the Albert Institute of 1867, designed by George Gilbert Scott, and its extension, the Victoria Galleries (1889), without compromising the integrity of the Grade A-listed structure. A new, accessible entrance has been formed by punching through a Gothic window, creating a glazed lobby and rotating the orientation of the building to foster a sense of arrival. New circulation, including a boldly contemporary sculptural stairway and lift, creates a legible route to the finely restored galleries behind. Altering the orientation of the building enabled the creation of a small hard-landscaped plaza at the front. The McManus is a triumph for a city that has excelled in building for the arts.

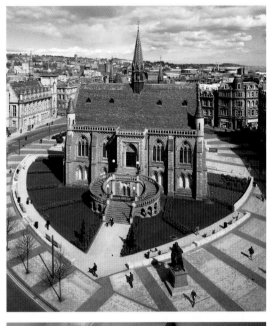

RAASAY COMMUNITY HALL
RAASAY, INNER HEBRIDES

DUALCHAS BUILDING DESIGN

CLIENT: RAASAY COMMUNITY ASSOCIATION
STRUCTURAL ENGINEER: CAMPBELL OF DOUNE
SERVICES ENGINEER: JIM COOMBER
CONTRACTOR: DONALD MACKENZIE HEATING AND BUILDING CONTRACTORS
CONTRACT VALUE: £900,000
DATE OF COMPLETION: 2009
GROSS INTERNAL AREA: 438 SQ. M
IMAGES: ANDREW LEE

Raasay has a small population but the same needs as any other community. The commission was for a multi-use hall, and the solution is a simple building formed by over-cladding a very large new shed with an untreated larch rainscreen, left to weather to a silvery grey. By using the slope of the site and creating separate entrances to upper and lower halls, the building avoids the expensive infrastructure and potential maintenance problems of a lift. The internal spaces are predominantly lined with wood. A ground-source heat pump with heat recovery minimizes energy use. The glazing of the front elevation ensures that users have a view of the constantly changing light and weather, of the sea and sky, and of the blue mountains of the Isle of Skye.

SCOTSTOUN HOUSE
SOUTH QUEENSFERRY, EDINBURGH

HAA DESIGN

CLIENT: ARUP GROUP
STRUCTURAL/SERVICES ENGINEER: ARUP SCOTLAND
CONTRACTOR: ASHWOOD SCOTLAND
CONTRACT VALUE: £3,500,000
DATE OF COMPLETION: JUNE 2010
GROSS INTERNAL AREA: 1682 SQ. M
IMAGES: ALAN MCTEER

The brief was to adapt and extend the Grade B-listed Scotstoun
House, the exemplary 'pavilion in the park', created as offices
for Ove Arup & Partners by Peter Foggo in 1963. The original
building, a single-storey construction of concrete, steel and
glass, has been adapted to accommodate contemporary working
patterns. A new, linear extension sits alongside, connecting with
the historic garden wall and directly abutting the existing pavilion,
which it complements rather than imitates. It draws on the
archaeology of its site and the simple elegance of the existing
building to create a new, adaptable office environment, human in
scale, energy-efficient (with a BREEAM 'Excellent' rating) and
welcoming – a fitting advertisement for a practice that has
proved itself on the world stage over two generations.

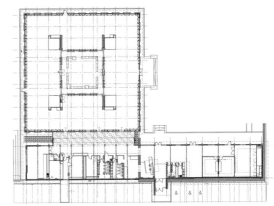

Floor plan

SHETTLESTON HOUSING ASSOCIATION OFFICES
PETTIGREW STREET, SHETTLESTON, GLASGOW

ELDER & CANNON ARCHITECTS

CLIENT: SHETTLESTON HOUSING ASSOCIATION
STRUCTURAL ENGINEER: THE STRUCTURAL PARTNERSHIP
SERVICES ENGINEER: HULLEY & KIRKWOOD CONSULTING ENGINEERS
CONTRACTOR: WAVERLY BUILDERS
CONTRACT VALUE: £1,900,000
DATE OF COMPLETION: JANUARY 2010
GROSS INTERNAL AREA: 1500 SQ. M
IMAGES: ANDREW LEE

The reworking of the existing early twentieth-century Cooperative Halls, and their extension to provide additional reception, meeting and administrative accommodation, bring together two distinct forms with aesthetics a century apart. The extension is an uncompromising and refreshing answer. Following the iconic five-bay rhythm of the existing block, its clearly delineated frame is pulled up to align with the eaves of the old. This compromises neither building, and leads to a development with great integrity. Extending the frame of the extension also adds a roof terrace to the facilities for staff. The clutter of the original spaces has been cleared, and timber pods and glass meeting rooms inserted. This is an exceptional work of affordable architecture, true to its time and place.

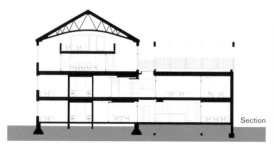

Section

SPEIRS LOCKS STUDIOS
GARSCUBE ROAD, GLASGOW

MALCOLM FRASER ARCHITECTS

CLIENT: ROYAL SCOTTISH ACADEMY OF MUSIC AND DRAMA
STRUCTURAL ENGINEER: STRUER CONSULTING ENGINEERS
SERVICES ENGINEER: ACTS PARTNERSHIP
CONTRACTOR: THOMAS JOHNSTONE
CONTRACT VALUE: £3,250,000
DATE OF COMPLETION: AUGUST 2010
GROSS INTERNAL AREA: 3480 SQ. M
IMAGES: DAVID MORRIS

Four nondescript 1980s portal-frame buildings have been skilfully and economically transformed into new technical teaching areas, including design studios, teaching rooms, a wardrobe department and paint, timber and stage workshops, for the Royal Scottish Academy of Music and Drama. It is a strongly detailed transformation with an industrial aesthetic. Circulation is organized on two levels, giving views down to the workshops from the upper storey. A separate entrance leads to four new, naturally lit studios for students of contemporary ballet and musical theatre. The building has been re-roofed, and new windows and profiled cladding further enhance its energy efficiency. A large, brightly painted sign attached directly to the existing brickwork marks the advent of an important new cultural asset for this area of Glasgow.

STRATHEDEN MENTAL HEALTH UNIT, STRATHEDEN HOSPITAL
CUPAR, FIFE

RICHARD MURPHY ARCHITECTS

CLIENT: NHS FIFE
STRUCTURAL ENGINEER: URS CORPORATION
SERVICES ENGINEER: CAPITA SYMONDS
CONTRACTOR: INTERSERVE
CONTRACT VALUE: £5,000,000
DATE OF COMPLETION: MAY 2010
GROSS INTERNAL AREA: 2300 SQ. M
IMAGES: GRAEME ARMET

The result of close cooperation between architect, client and nursing staff, this project is a contemporary day-lit environment designed to improve the well-being and state of mind of residents. It is far removed from the historic ward facilities it replaces. Two single-storey pavilions set in gardens cater for individuals with varying levels of neurodegeneration, with eighteen and twenty-four bedrooms respectively, all en suite. All this has been achieved at a domestic scale, with circulation spaces that enable both quiet contemplation and indoor and outdoor exercise. Both buildings contain rooms ranged around garden courtyards with water features, and both take advantage of the views of open countryside. Despite significant security requirements, the unit provides comfortable, calming accommodation within a light and welcoming environment.

TIGH-NA-CLADACH
BULLWOOD ROAD, DUNOON

GOKAY DEVECI CHARTERED ARCHITECT

CLIENT: FYNE INITIATIVES
STRUCTURAL ENGINEER: RAMAGE YOUNG PARTNERSHIP
CONTRACTOR: JOHN BROWN (STRONE)
CONTRACT VALUE: £2,400,000
DATE OF COMPLETION: APRIL 2010
GROSS INTERNAL AREA: 1438 SQ. M
IMAGES: ANDREW LEE

This colourful development of fourteen affordable homes is the first social housing in the United Kingdom to be accredited by the German Passivhaus Institut, attesting to its rigorous energy standards. While first impressions may be of a simple row of over-scaled two-storey beach huts, it is in fact an ingenious mix of interlocking flats and houses, the first-floor flats enhanced by roof terraces on the link sections. The construction is of prefabricated super-insulated I-beam roof and walls, finished with render on blockwork. The development includes a small workshop, providing education for people with special needs as part of the management of the woodland behind. The project serves an important social purpose and reflects the grain of the town, while adding a refreshing splash of colour.

THE WHITE HOUSE
GRISHIPOL, ISLE OF COLL, INNER HEBRIDES

WT ARCHITECTURE

CLIENTS: ALEX AND SEONAID MACLEAN
STRUCTURAL ENGINEER: DAVID NARRO ASSOCIATES
CONTRACTOR: SPEY BUILDING AND JOINERY
CONTRACT VALUE: £735,000
DATE OF COMPLETION: JULY 2010
GROSS INTERNAL AREA: 267 SQ. M
IMAGES: ANDREW LEE
SHORTLISTED FOR THE STEPHEN LAWRENCE PRIZE

The architect and the clients sought to create a contemporary
family home incorporating the listed shell of a small eighteenth-
century ruined house. The partial reuse of this existing house
delineates the new development, which is composed of two
accommodation blocks connected by a glazed living–dining
space. While the ruin has been consolidated and parts are
incorporated within the new building, the separation of historic
and contemporary is clear. A new timber structure perches on
a substantial drystone wall, built on old enclosure lines and
reusing stone from the site – a lightweight break with the
local vernacular that is nevertheless grounded in its robust
landscape and tradition. The house thus sits comfortably in
this extraordinarily beautiful landscape.

CARNATHAN LANE
DONAGHADEE

TWENTY TWO OVER SEVEN

CLIENTS: ROBERT AND BERNIE SERVICE
STRUCTURAL ENGINEER: IVOR ARMSTRONG ASSOCIATES
CONTRACTOR: GAVIN BOYD
CONTRACT VALUE: £330,000
DATE OF COMPLETION: MARCH 2010
GROSS INTERNAL AREA: 350 SQ. M
IMAGES: AIDAN MCGRATH

Carnathan Lane is a well-balanced and thoughtful plan, and offers a fresh interpretation of a Celtic vernacular. The exterior form retains a memory of the 1970s house that previously stood on the site. The front elevation refers to Mackay Hugh Baillie Scott with the well-placed horizontal windows on the ground and first floors. The single-storey elements at the rear, with one pitched roof and one flat, create private external garden rooms that reflect the great consideration given to the relationship between the house and its landscape. The detail is consistent, robust and thoroughly executed throughout, from the timber staircase to the bespoke doors and windows, and from the fine roof to the external rendering. Porcelain floors and the use of oak give the house a sense of high quality that belies its modest budget.

55/02

COCK STOOR, LAKESIDE WAY, KIELDER WATER & FOREST PARK, NORTHUMBERLAND

SIXTEEN* (MAKERS) @ THE BARTLETT UCL

CLIENT: KIELDER PARTNERSHIP
CONTRACTOR: STAHLBOGEN
CONTRACT VALUE: £60,000
DATE OF COMPLETION: JULY 2009
GROSS INTERNAL AREA: 30 SQ. M
IMAGE: SIXTEEN (MAKERS)* @ THE BARTLETT UCL

This piece, the name of which refers to its grid reference, takes a worthy place among the architectural and art treasures of Kielder Forest, several of which have already won RIBA Awards. The shelter can be seen in tantalizing glimpses from afar, but its full impact is not revealed until the traveller arrives at the site through the maze of paths. Constructed from thick folded steel that has been painstakingly and accurately drawn, shaped and fabricated, this bold, red, mysterious piece is an enigmatic resting point at the tip of a spit of land jutting into the lake. It echoes the relationship between the verticality of the trees and the horizontality of the water. The smooth, brightly coloured, inorganic nature of the steel stands in dramatic contrast to the mature woodland that surrounds it.

APOLLO PAVILION
PETERLEE, COUNTY DURHAM

BURNS ARCHITECTS

CLIENT: DURHAM COUNTY COUNCIL
STRUCTURAL/ELECTRICAL ENGINEER: DTA CONSULTING ENGINEERS
CONTRACTOR: FREYSSINET
CONTRACT VALUE: £400,000
DATE OF COMPLETION: JULY 2009
IMAGES: BURNS ARCHITECTS (CENTRE; BOTTOM); HAROLD WILSON (TOP)

The original Apollo Pavilion, designed by Victor Pasmore and
built as part of Peterlee's social housing development, is not
so much an important one-off piece as a gathering of bold
architectural ideas manifested in the delightful sculptural form
of reinforced concrete. Its extensive academic and methodical
restoration has been undertaken with a great deal of precision
and care. The pavilion bridges a flowing, curved pond at one
end, revealing a series of open and partially enclosed spaces
from which to enjoy views across the park. This combination of
reopening the piece for people to enjoy and restoring the whole
sculpted landscape allows the pavilion to be re-embraced by
both its surroundings and its visitors.

KNOP LAW PRIMARY SCHOOL
HILLHEAD PARKWAY, WESTERHOPE,
NEWCASTLE UPON TYNE

ADP

CLIENT: AURA
CONTRACTOR: SIR ROBERT MCALPINE
CONTRACT VALUE: £7,400,000
DATE OF COMPLETION: SEPTEMBER 2010
GROSS INTERNAL AREA: 2535 SQ. M
IMAGES: ANDREW HEPTINSTALL

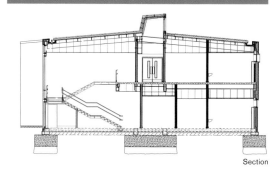

Section

Knop Law may well turn out to represent an important moment in time, marking a return to core values in respect of the way children are nurtured and taught in intuitive and ambitious surroundings. An atmosphere of ease yet formality permeates all the activities of the school, engendered at least in part by the architecture; the aspiration to decency and inquisitive thought in the design will surely find its way into the minds of the users of this delightful place. Expression of use has been distilled to a few honest elements. Vertical white render forms a blade of division between wings, and classrooms are divided by horizontal planes of glass, clear balustrades or metal cladding. Colour also provides the narrative to differentiate zones of use.

MILLFIELD HOUSE VISITOR CENTRE
JESMOND DENE, NEWCASTLE UPON TYNE

MOSEDALE GILLATT ARCHITECTS

CLIENT: NEWCASTLE CITY COUNCIL
STRUCTURAL ENGINEER: PATRICK PARSONS
SERVICES ENGINEER: SINE CONSULTING
CONTRACTOR: ROK BUILDING
CONTRACT VALUE: £1,460,000
DATE OF COMPLETION: JUNE 2010
GROSS INTERNAL AREA: 960 SQ. M
IMAGES: IONA OWEN

The project extends an existing building and sits at the focal point of Jesmond Dene, a linear park that has served generations of visiting families. Seen from all directions it is a well-considered response to the park: forms, colours, textures and volumes establish a consistent narrative with their complementary pieces, which include a footbridge and an animal shelter. The most striking example is the contrast of the thin Cor-ten verticals of the bridge structure with the curved timber cladding on the upper floor of the visitor centre. The sedum roof and rainwater collection systems announce the building's environmental credentials, but the real magic is in its relationship with the old building and with the events that take place in the park.

CHARLES CARTER BUILDING, LANCASTER UNIVERSITY
LANCASTER

JOHN MCASLAN + PARTNERS

CLIENT: LANCASTER UNIVERSITY
STRUCTURAL ENGINEERS: SKM ANTHONY HUNT; WYG ENGINEERING
SERVICES ENGINEER: HOARE LEA
CONTRACTOR: GALLIFORD TRY CONSTRUCTION NORTH
CONTRACT VALUE: £6,500,000
DATE OF COMPLETION: FEBRUARY 2011
GROSS INTERNAL AREA: 3995 SQ. M
IMAGES: HUFTON & CROW – VIEW

This new management school displays a simple architecture that cleverly combines a colonnade, giant orders, deep recesses and flush seamless detail. The single-minded pursuit externally of the possibilities of contemporary brick technology is complemented internally by the exposed concrete frame. These two materials give the building a sense of grandeur and permanence that is all too rare in contemporary educational buildings. The use of natural light and ventilation and the generous atrium ensure that the building not only has personality but also is robust, flexible and enjoyable. Its simple form, material clarity and environmental strategy (of thermal mass, natural ventilation and daylight) set a new standard for the university in terms of place-making, the provision of space and care for the planet.

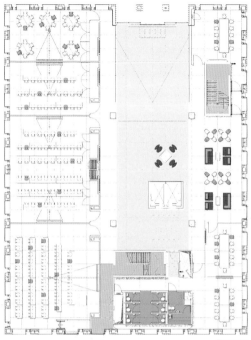

Floor plan

HEATING INFRASTRUCTURE PROJECT, UNIVERSITY OF LIVERPOOL
ASHTON STREET, LIVERPOOL

LEVITT BERNSTEIN

CLIENT: UNIVERSITY OF LIVERPOOL
STRUCTURAL ENGINEER: CURTINS CONSULTING
M&E ENGINEER: NIFES CONSULTING GROUP
CONTRACTOR: EMCOR
CONTRACT VALUE: £22,000,000
DATE OF COMPLETION: JANUARY 2010
GROSS INTERNAL AREA: 1060 SQ. M
IMAGES: EDDIE JACOBS

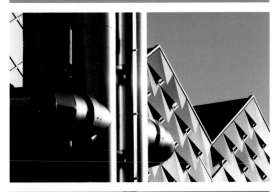

This project continues the noble architectural tradition of the boiler house as urban monument: glazed gable ends reveal glimpses of the power that hums within. The delightfully compact building sits neatly on its site and has an articulated roof form that cleverly makes reference to the architecture of its listed neighbours while concealing the chillers. This play of geometry is complemented by an elegantly conceived and executed fish-scale skin that articulates the otherwise blank façades and allows cross ventilation. Importantly, the building is more than a clever architectural enclosure: the energy generated within provides much of Liverpool University's needs. This project is a complete tale of making new, repairing old and conserving resources.

LAWSON PARK
EAST OF LAKE, CONISTON, CUMBRIA

SUTHERLAND HUSSEY ARCHITECTS

CLIENT: GRIZEDALE ARTS (ADAM SUTHERLAND, DIRECTOR)
STRUCTURAL ENGINEER: BLEASDALE WAND
SERVICES ENGINEER: DAVID ELEY ASSOCIATES
CONTRACTOR: LECK CONSTRUCTION
CONTRACT VALUE: £910,000
DATE OF COMPLETION: MAY 2009
GROSS INTERNAL AREA: 392 SQ. M
IMAGES: SUTHERLAND HUSSEY ARCHITECTS

An ancient farmhouse, outbuildings and gardens on an isolated
hillside in the Lake District have been refurbished to provide both
a home for the warden and accommodation and workspaces for
visiting artists. A split-level section resolves the meeting of old
and new, and provides enjoyable vistas and connections between
the areas for living, working and eating. The volumes created
are celebrated by boldly sculpted ceilings that define space
with light. The limited existing apertures in the original walls are
similarly sculpted on the inside to draw the eye to the magnificent
views. This is an ongoing project in which a skilful series of
architectural insertions enable, inspire and respond to the making
of and thinking about art.

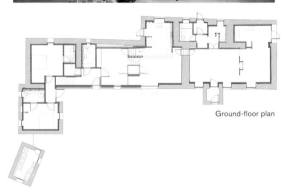

Ground-floor plan

LOVE SHACK
CUNSEY, AMBLESIDE, CUMBRIA

SUTHERLAND HUSSEY ARCHITECTS

CLIENTS: KAREN GUTHRIE AND ADAM SUTHERLAND
CONTRACTOR: SELF-BUILD
CONTRACT VALUE: £100,805
DATE OF COMPLETION: OCTOBER 2009
GROSS INTERNAL AREA: 41 SQ. M
IMAGES: KAREN GUTHRIE

This intriguingly named rural retreat is a delightful essay in doing much with very little. The two rooms are anchored to a deck that is reached via a stepped ramp and which defines a courtyard and views of the lake and hills. This highly skilled architectural piece also demonstrates how a small domestic residence might touch the earth lightly: both literally, as it floats on piles, and practically, as it is clad in boards from the wood in which it sits, carefully placed among mature trees. This building works with its locale by preserving what is there, and exploiting for pleasure the local resources of timber, topography and views. What is more, it is available to rent.

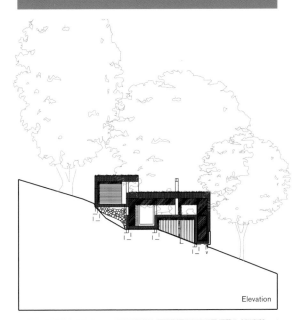

Elevation

Elevation

TRAFFORD COLLEGE LEARNING RESOURCE CENTRE
MANCHESTER ROAD, WEST TIMPERLEY, ALTRINCHAM

STEPHENSON BELL

CLIENT: TRAFFORD COLLEGE
STRUCTURAL/SERVICES ENGINEER: WYG ENGINEERING
CONTRACTOR: MILLER CONSTRUCTION
CONTRACT VALUE: £25,000,000
DATE OF COMPLETION: FEBRUARY 2011
GROSS INTERNAL AREA: 8960 SQ. M
IMAGES: DANIEL HOPKINSON – ARCAID

The final phase in the rethinking of this educational campus demonstrates the long-term potential of generous volumes, simple organization and a commitment both to strategic design and to fine detail. The building is entered through a new atrium from a soon-to-be-completed public square that addresses the city and proclaims the project's importance not only to staff and students but also to the wider community. Beyond this important arrival and organizing space, beautifully detailed teaching rooms lend daylight through generous windows to bright corridors. In the most public rooms, such as the library, the carefully shaded picture windows are wherever possible complemented by clerestories that throw light deep into the plan while allowing glimpses of the sky and the city.

GRANARY WHARF MASTERPLAN
LEEDS

CAREYJONES CHAPMANTOLCHER; CZWG ARCHITECTS; ALLIES AND MORRISON ARCHITECTS

CLIENT: ISIS WATERSIDE REGENERATION
STRUCTURAL ENGINEERS: BURO HAPPOLD; RAMBOLL UK
SERVICES ENGINEER: AECOM
CONTRACTORS: ARDMORE CONSTRUCTION; LAING O'ROURKE
CONTRACT VALUE: £72,000,000
DATE OF COMPLETION: AUGUST 2010
IMAGES: HUFTON & CROW – VIEW

CareyJones ChapmanTolcher's masterplan for the underused wharf site between the River Aire and the Leeds–Liverpool Canal envisaged a twenty-one-storey cylindrical residential tower, Candle House, which the firm delivered, as well as the Mint Hotel by Allies and Morrison Architects and a residential block, Waterman's Place, by CZWG Architects. The design code establishes the predominance of brick in a strong palette of materials and the rigorous application of the material (in the window reveals, for example) across the site. The choice of brick is entirely appropriate to the strongly historic context, resulting in a series of enjoyable, subtle and elegant elevations and usable spaces. The three schemes complement one another in form and materials, although their geometric expressions are very different. The next phase of the scheme will connect it directly to the railway station, with the intention of increasing footfall.

HESLINGTON EAST CAMPUS MASTERPLAN, THE UNIVERSITY OF YORK
YORK

BDP

CLIENT: THE UNIVERSITY OF YORK
STRUCTURAL/CIVIL ENGINEER: AECOM
SERVICES ENGINEER: ARUP
CONTRACTOR: BAM CONSTRUCTION UK
CONTRACT VALUE: £107,300,000
DATE OF COMPLETION: DECEMBER 2009
GROSS INTERNAL AREA: 41,295 SQ. M
IMAGES: MARTINE HAMILTON KNIGHT – ARCAID

The site, acquired in 2007 and masterplanned by BDP, is adjacent to the 1960s university campus and already accommodates Goodricke College, the Computer Science, Theatre and Film & Television buildings, and the Law and Management schools. Eventually it will double the size of the university. The landscape strategy sets out a structure that is dominated not by highways and parking, but by the movement of pedestrians and cyclists through a series of vistas, routes, edges and shortcuts. The success of the masterplan lies in the subtlety of these spaces and the arrangement of the buildings, the geometry of which creates protective microclimates. Each building has its own distinctive landscape setting and 'inner world', which balances the need for intimacy with the civic nature of the masterplan.

Elevation

SANDAL MAGNA COMMUNITY PRIMARY SCHOOL
BELLE VUE ROAD, WAKEFIELD

SARAH WIGGLESWORTH ARCHITECTS

CLIENT: WAKEFIELD COUNCIL
STRUCTURAL ENGINEER: TECHNIKER
SERVICES ENGINEER: MAX FORDHAM
CONTRACTOR: ALLENBUILD NORTH EAST
CONTRACT VALUE: £5,000,000
DATE OF COMPLETION: SEPTEMBER 2010
GROSS INTERNAL AREA: 1769 SQ. M
IMAGES: MARK HADDEN PHOTOGRAPHY
LONGLISTED FOR THE RIBA STIRLING PRIZE

Sarah Wigglesworth's first new-build school is exemplary in many ways. The diagram is clear: three fingers of accommodation with play spaces in between. The rigour of the design has resulted in a highly functional but exciting building, simple in plan form but encouraging curiosity in its users. The services are integrated into the children's learning; the snaking copper sprinkler pipes and the flying service ducts, for example, encourage them to ask questions. The playfulness continues in the classrooms, with traffic lights indicating levels of CO_2. Then there are the transparent rainwater pipes and the 100 square metres of photovoltaic panels. The school deserves high praise for the quality of its design and for its functionality, sustainability and aesthetics, but most of all for the joy it brings to all its users.

SHARROW POINT
CEMETERY ROAD, SHEFFIELD

PROJECT ORANGE

CLIENT: NEAVERSONS
STRUCTURAL ENGINEERS: PROJECT DESIGN ASSOCIATES; ELLIOTT WOOD
    PARTNERSHIP
SERVICES ENGINEERS: SHEARSTONE MECHANICAL; CUBA CONSULTANTS
CONTRACT VALUE: £3,000,000
DATE OF COMPLETION: MARCH 2010
GROSS INTERNAL AREA: 3600 SQ. M
IMAGES: GARETH GARDNER

Project Orange's high-density scheme of town houses, flats and commercial units has been achieved at the remarkable cost of just £830 per square metre, and it doesn't show. Yorkshire stone is used where the buildings face a conservation area, but turn a corner and the palette changes to white render, black-stained timber and pre-patinated zinc. Perhaps the greatest interest, however, lies in the two different house plans. Both are designed with dynamic cross sections and generous balconies and terraces, but in one a promenade route meanders through the house, producing dramatic views while avoiding overlooking. Pulling the staircase close to the gable end also makes for a close connection with the courtyard. This is a refreshing departure from the typical suburban development in Sheffield.

Ground-floor plan

BLUE DOOR
FAR HILL, LLANISHEN, CHEPSTOW

HALL + BEDNARCZYK ARCHITECTS

CLIENTS: MR AND MRS M. MILLING
STRUCTURAL ENGINEER: STEVE MORGAN ASSOCIATES
SERVICES ENGINEER: HOLLOWAY PARTNERSHIP
CONTRACTOR: ROB MACCORMAC
CONTRACT VALUE: £430,000
DATE OF COMPLETION: JANUARY 2010
GROSS INTERNAL AREA: 256 SQ. M
IMAGES: LEIGHTON MORRIS

Blue Door is a contemporary house designed for retired clients in
the Wye valley and cut into a steep, elevated site. The retaining
wall incorporates a rooflight, allowing illumination deep into the
building. Clad externally in oxidized-copper-coated ceramic tiles
and horizontal cedar boarding, the house has an oversailing
timber monocoque roof in zinc; three double-glazed curved
corner windows enhance the building's fluid form. A ground-
source heat pump augmented by a heat-recovery system
provides warmth in cold weather. This confident piece of
architecture has provided the clients with a visually quiet and
delightfully understated home. Disappointingly, though, it doesn't
have a blue door.

CARDIFF SCHOOL OF MANAGEMENT, UNIVERSITY OF WALES INSTITUTE, CARDIFF

WESTERN AVENUE, CARDIFF

AUSTIN-SMITH:LORD

CLIENT: UNIVERSITY OF WALES INSTITUTE, CARDIFF
CONTRACTOR: WILLMOTT DIXON
CONTRACT VALUE: £13,100,000
DATE OF COMPLETION: SEPTEMBER 2010
GROSS INTERNAL AREA: 8008 SQ. M
IMAGES: MORLEY VON STERNBERG – ARCAID

On a long, narrow site in a conservation area, adjacent to Llandaff Cathedral, the client required a signature building of high architectural quality, targeting a BREEAM 'Excellent' rating. The building is organized as two distinct elements flanking a large circulation atrium. A three-storey wing houses the main entrance – under the angled soffit that is the pitched floor of the auditorium above – administration, a hospitality suite and academic workspaces. The lower-ground floor, with its cladding of blue Staffordshire brick, acts as a strong base for the upper levels, which are clad in pre-oxidized copper. Inside, the building is very cleanly and elegantly detailed. The linear timber-clad staircase creates a positive vertical element, more like a large piece of crafted furniture than a flight of stairs.

MOSTYN GALLERY
VAUGHAN STREET, LLANDUDNO

ELLIS WILLIAMS ARCHITECTS

CLIENT: MOSTYN GALLERY
CONTRACTOR: RLD CONSTRUCTION
CONTRACT VALUE: £5,100,000
DATE OF COMPLETION: MAY 2010
GROSS INTERNAL AREA: 2000 SQ. M
IMAGES: HÉLÈNE BINET

The Mostyn Gallery of 1901, with its elegant brick-and-stone façade and delightful linked steel-and-glass canopy, has been extended and refurbished, more than doubling its size. A former retail unit became available during the design process, and was incorporated to free up the plan, allowing one of the new galleries to face the street and announce the building's function. The architect has cleverly arranged three new gallery spaces, one of which is double height with a series of angled rooflights. The light playing on the walls and drawing out the texture of the shuttering softens any hardness. This confident addition to the Welsh art scene refreshes without overwhelming the works themselves.

STUDENTS' UNION, UNIVERSITY OF GLAMORGAN
RADWAY, TREFOREST, PONTYPRIDD

RIO ARCHITECTS

CLIENT: UNIVERSITY OF GLAMORGAN ESTATES DEPARTMENT
STRUCTURAL ENGINEER: SHEAR DESIGN
SERVICES ENGINEER: MCCANN & PARTNERS
CONTRACTOR: VINCI CONSTRUCTION UK
CONTRACT VALUE: £4,000,000
DATE OF COMPLETION: SEPTEMBER 2010
GROSS INTERNAL AREA: 2500 SQ. M
IMAGES: RICHARD ROBERTS

Located near the entrance to the campus, on a narrow, steeply sloping site, the new Students' Union required a lot to be squeezed in. Despite the physical constraints, the architect has achieved a fully inclusive building, even finding room for external terraces. The palette of materials – slate walls, extensive glazing with timber louvres, zinc cladding and rendered surfaces – is used simply yet clearly, with the stone forming the base and glazed façades floating above. The internal sequence of spaces makes it a pleasing building to explore, with a triple-height staircase acting as the pivot around which the plan rotates. The accommodation provides everything students require: meeting spaces, relaxation areas, a cafe, bars, administration, a nightclub and performing venue and a shop.

TY HEDFAN
PONTFAEN, BRECON, POWYS

FEATHERSTONE YOUNG

CLIENTS: JEREMY YOUNG AND SARAH FEATHERSTONE
STRUCTURAL ENGINEER: TECHNIKER
CONTRACTOR: OSBORNE BUILDERS
CONTRACT VALUE: £550,000
DATE OF COMPLETION: AUGUST 2010
GROSS INTERNAL AREA: 233 SQ. M
IMAGES: TIM BROTHERTON (CENTRE; BOTTOM LEFT); FEATHERSTONE YOUNG
    (TOP; BOTTOM RIGHT)
SHORTLISTED FOR THE RIBA MANSER MEDAL AND THE STEPHEN LAWRENCE
    PRIZE

Ty Hedfan, or 'Hovering House', cantilevers over its site, cleverly avoiding the planning constraint on building within 7 metres of the nearby river. The design, which references the traditional Welsh long house, uses a striking and expressive 9-metre-tall drystone wall as the knuckle between the rectangular form of the main house and the bedroom wing, buried in the hillside under a green sedum roof. The best views are from the cantilevered living room, where one feels as though one is among the trees. The wing has generous full-height glazing and three rooflights, allowing daylight to permeate the deeper parts. The rooflights are intriguingly detailed, resembling wooden cattle troughs in a field.

UNIVERSITY OF WALES, NEWPORT, CITY CAMPUS
USK WAY, NEWPORT

BDP

CLIENT: UNIVERSITY OF WALES, NEWPORT
STRUCTURAL ENGINEER: OPUS INTERNATIONAL CONSULTANTS
CONTRACTOR: MOTT MACDONALD
CONTRACT VALUE: £25,200,000
DATE OF COMPLETION: JANUARY 2011
GROSS INTERNAL AREA: 12,500 SQ. M
IMAGES: MARTINE HAMILTON KNIGHT – ARCAID

Conceived as part of a masterplan for the University of Wales to create a new campus beside the River Usk (with a secondary aim of regenerating the waterfront), this new building gathers together the Business, Technology, Art, Design and Media disciplines into a single collaborative environment under a large all-encompassing roof. Accommodation includes heavily serviced sound and television studios, screening theatres, lecture theatres, learning support, exhibition space, teaching studios and academic offices. The building is well planned and fluidly knits together diverse uses in a positive manner. Academic buildings have to earn their keep these days, hence the public internal street, which, as well as giving access to the performance spaces, hosts student exhibitions and external revenue-earning exhibitions.

WISE, CENTRE FOR ALTERNATIVE TECHNOLOGY
MACHYNLLETH, POWYS

DAVID LEA AND PAT BORER ARCHITECTS

CLIENT: CENTRE FOR ALTERNATIVE TECHNOLOGY
CONTRACTOR: IAN SNEADE
CONTRACT VALUE: £4,500,000
DATE OF COMPLETION: JUNE 2010
GROSS INTERNAL AREA: 2000 SQ. M
IMAGES: PAT BORER (TOP); TIMOTHY SOAR (CENTRE AND BOTTOM)
LONGLISTED FOR THE RIBA STIRLING PRIZE

WISE (Wales Institute for Sustainable Education) is constructed from materials with low embodied energy: a glulam timber frame, hempcrete walls, rammed earth, lime renders, slate, cork, home-grown timber flooring and natural paints and stains. It is well insulated and airtight, with solar-tube arrays and photovoltaic panels on the roof, and heat-recovery systems, and is connected to a bio-fuel combined heat and power plant. The naturally ventilated accommodation is arranged around courtyards, and includes a restaurant, a bar, a foyer, a 200-seat lecture theatre, offices, teaching rooms and twenty-four en-suite bedrooms. Today the word 'sustainability' is often used glibly; this project does not merely live up to the centre's mission, but does so with quiet confidence. Many such buildings ram home their credentials, but this building does not and, as a result, is a delight.

TEENAGE CANCER TRUST WARD, BIRMINGHAM CHILDREN'S HOSPITAL
STEELHOUSE LANE, BIRMINGHAM

LIFSCHUTZ DAVIDSON SANDILANDS

CLIENT: SIMON DAVIES, TEENAGE CANCER TRUST
STRUCTURAL ENGINEER: HEYNE TILLETT STEEL
SERVICES ENGINEER: NORMAN DISNEY & YOUNG
CONTRACTOR: VINCI CONSTRUCTION UK
CONTRACT VALUE: £2,200,000
DATE OF COMPLETION: JANUARY 2010
GROSS INTERNAL AREA: 400 SQ. M
IMAGES: CHRIS GASCOIGNE – VIEW

This lightweight single-storey structure perches over the Accident & Emergency department and the fracture clinic. It is situated in a busy and chaotic part of the city, cut off by roads and surrounded by hospital buildings of varying dates and styles, all embracing one other. The architect has created an oasis of peace and calm while meeting the very specific and stringent requirements of the NHS. The attention to detail and to colour is remarkable. The entry corridor, with its free forms carved out of the thick internal wall on one side, is witty and enjoyable, and makes for a pleasant approach to the ward. It is a sad reflection, perhaps, but this does not feel like a typical NHS building.

Section

CRESWELL CRAGS MUSEUM AND VISITOR CENTRE
CRAGS ROAD, WELBECK, WORKSOP

OMI ARCHITECTS

CLIENT: CRESWELL CRAGS MUSEUM AND VISITOR CENTRE
STRUCTURAL/SERVICES ENGINEER: BURO HAPPOLD
CONTRACTOR: G.F. TOMLINSON BUILDING
CONTRACT VALUE: £3,800,000
DATE OF COMPLETION: JUNE 2009
GROSS INTERNAL AREA: 1285 SQ. M
IMAGES: DANIEL HOPKINSON – ARCAID

Located on a site replete with important archaeology, this appropriate and sensitive building is the gateway to an understanding of the history and culture of the region. The spatial arrangements are simply but carefully designed and detailed, with imaginative use of stone and timber. The building's relationship with the land and its use of section to move people down a natural change in level are handled well. Structure and the content easily complement each other: the exhibition is informative both for schoolchildren and for expert visitors, and topics of ecology and sustainability are addressed in a thoughtful manner. The attention to detail is carried through into the landscape with a playful bridge that encourages guests to explore the archaeology and the natural setting.

Upper-ground-floor plan

THE MEAT FACTORY
FELTON ROAD, THE MEADOWS, NOTTINGHAM

MARSH GROCHOWSKI ARCHITECTS

CLIENT: JUDY AND JULIAN MARSH
STRUCTURAL ENGINEER: PRICE & MYERS
SERVICES ENGINEER: BURO HAPPOLD
CONTRACTOR: SELF-BUILD
CONTRACT VALUE: £500,000
DATE OF COMPLETION: MAY 2010
GROSS INTERNAL AREA: 222 SQ. M
IMAGES: HANNAH MARSH (BOTTOM); MARSH GROCHOWSKI ARCHITECTS
    (TOP; CENTRE)

The Meat Factory is a domestic experiment in sustainable living in a deprived area of Nottingham, occupied by its architect owner, who is practising what he preaches. The house will, no doubt, act as a catalyst for change and the increased awareness of sustainability in the neighbourhood. It was built over a number of years, largely by the owner himself, and the design grew organically as he tried out ideas. Sometimes this was in response to the availability of materials, sometimes because another project had fallen through: the design of the glass bridge, for instance, was appropriated from an unbuilt scheme. There is a sense that this is a continuing process, and that the plan and even the elevations might evolve over time.

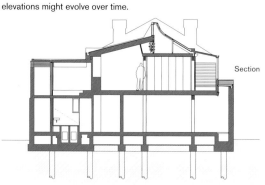

Section

NEWTON AND ARKWRIGHT BUILDINGS, NOTTINGHAM TRENT UNIVERSITY
GOLDSMITH STREET, NOTTINGHAM

HOPKINS ARCHITECTS

CLIENT: NOTTINGHAM TRENT UNIVERSITY
STRUCTURAL/SERVICES ENGINEER: ARUP
CONTRACTOR: BOWMER & KIRKLAND
CONTRACT VALUE: £90,000,000
DATE OF COMPLETION: MARCH 2010
GROSS INTERNAL AREA: 31,183 SQ. M
IMAGES: MARTINE HAMILTON KNIGHT – ARCAID

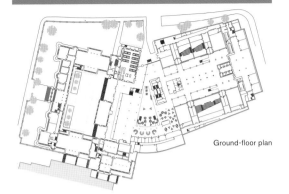

Ground-floor plan

Two historic buildings have been skilfully renovated to create a contemporary university facility. Entry to the ground floor is controlled from four axial points via a top-lit central space between the two buildings, making a complex series of spaces easily understandable and accessible. The quality of light offers a pleasant environment for multifunctional break-out spaces and relaxation and work areas appropriate to the learning environment. Glazed internal partitions create interest and transparency. The transition between new and old is seamless; the restoration work aimed to reuse as much of the building fabric as possible, exposing ceilings, façades and internal elevations that had been obscured for years.

Elevation

WOODLAND TRUST HEADQUARTERS
KEMPTON WAY, GRANTHAM

FEILDEN CLEGG BRADLEY STUDIOS

CLIENT: WOODLAND TRUST
STRUCTURAL ENGINEER: ATELIER ONE
SERVICES ENGINEER: MAX FORDHAM
CONTRACTOR: BOWMER & KIRKLAND
CONTRACT VALUE: £5,100,000
DATE OF COMPLETION: OCTOBER 2010
GROSS INTERNAL AREA: 2728 SQ. M
IMAGES: PETER COOK – VIEW

The form of the building responds in a creative way to the constraints and opportunities of the industrial estate on which it is situated. The full-height timber siding and window slots emphasize the verticality and produce a strongly graphic image for the Woodland Trust. The generous circulation space at the heart of the building and the airy open-plan offices create a pleasant work environment. The use of timber for both structure and cladding was a given, of course, but the architect has hung lightweight concrete elements from the ceiling in order to boost the mass of the building and hence save energy. A simple palette of materials and colours generates a consistent and unified ambience throughout the project.

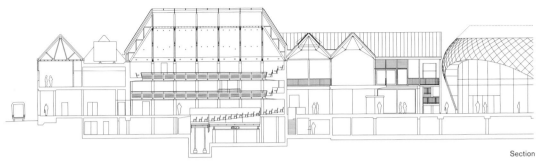

Section

THE APEX
ARC, BURY ST EDMUNDS

HOPKINS ARCHITECTS

CLIENT: ST EDMUNDSBURY BOROUGH COUNCIL
STRUCTURAL ENGINEER: WSP GROUP
SERVICES ENGINEER: AECOM
CONTRACTOR: HAYMILLS
CONTRACT VALUE: £15,000,000
DATE OF COMPLETION: SEPTEMBER 2010
GROSS INTERNAL AREA: 29,000 SQ. M
IMAGES: MORLEY VON STERNBERG – ARCAID
LONGLISTED FOR THE RIBA STIRLING PRIZE

The retail-led route to the regeneration of our historic towns requires civic leadership, strong architects and the right choice of development partner. In Bury St Edmunds all are in evidence. Instead of the customary trail of excuses and missed opportunities, planning restrictions, cost-cutting, procurement problems and compromises demanded by retailers leading down the path of least resistance and producing general mediocrity, a new town centre has been designed of which all its citizens can be proud. More than 25,000 square metres of retail, sixty-two flats and a new civic auditorium have all been delivered through a simple masterplan based on a new public square. The building language is clear and consistent, with a simple form that is highly appropriate to its setting.

THE BALANCING BARN
THORINGTON, SUFFOLK

MVRDV WITH MOLE ARCHITECTS

CLIENT: LIVING ARCHITECTURE
STRUCTURAL/SERVICES ENGINEER: JANE WERNICK ASSOCIATES
CONTRACTOR: SEAMANS BUILDING
CONTRACT VALUE: CONFIDENTIAL
DATE OF COMPLETION: OCTOBER 2010
GROSS INTERNAL AREA: 210 SQ. M
IMAGES: LIVING ARCHITECTURE (TOP AND CENTRE); EDMUND SUMNER –
    VIEW (BOTTOM)
SHORTLISTED FOR THE RIBA MANSER MEDAL

The house, one of Alain de Botton's Living Architecture projects, was designed as a holiday home for people who wish to have a dialogue with landscape. Instead, it has a voyeuristic character whereby visitors gaze out on, rather than engage with, their surroundings. As a place to visit rather than live in, it develops the idea of mismatch and imbalance. The consistent use of ash on walls, floors and ceilings gives a carved quality to the interior that is cleverly at odds with the slight defections that remind visitors they are suspended in mid-air. Buildings that evoke such powerful feelings of obscure but pleasurable unease are rare, and the Balancing Barn hits the mark in a very unusual way.

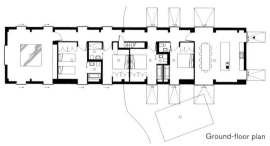

Ground-floor plan

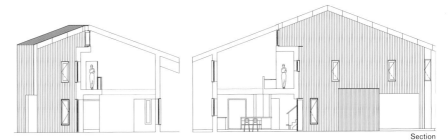

Section

BAVENT HOUSE
REYDON, SUFFOLK

HUDSON ARCHITECTS

CLIENTS: LUCY AND RICHARD TURVILL
STRUCTURAL ENGINEER: J.P. CHICK & PARTNERS
CONTRACTOR: ROBERT NORMAN ASSOCIATES
CONTRACT VALUE: £600,000
DATE OF COMPLETION: AUGUST 2010
GROSS INTERNAL AREA: 290 SQ. M
IMAGES: JAMES BRITTAIN – VIEW

The success of the television series *Grand Designs* has spawned a new generation of would-be housebuilders who are prepared to fight the planners to create their dream homes in idyllic rural settings. Some architects, meanwhile, have become interested in a contemporary vernacular that is respectful of a rural tradition yet expressive in its ideas about making a home. This new approach, without any hint of pastiche, can be proudly passed on to future generations. Bavent House is part of the local vernacular, being a mix of timber and metal cladding expressed through a series of pitched forms that could easily have been modified over time. There is an intelligence to this house that has less to do with the 'grand' and much more to do with the 'design'.

CENTRE FOR COMPETITIVE CREATIVE DESIGN (C4D), CRANFIELD UNIVERSITY
CRANFIELD, BEDFORDSHIRE

NÍALL MCLAUGHLIN ARCHITECTS

CLIENT: CRANFIELD UNIVERSITY
STRUCTURAL ENGINEER: PRICE & MYERS
SERVICES ENGINEER: MICHAEL POPPER ASSOCIATES
CONTRACTOR: KIER MARRIOTT
CONTRACT VALUE: £1,250,000
DATE OF COMPLETION: AUGUST 2010
GROSS INTERNAL AREA: 300 SQ. M
IMAGES: NICK KANE – ARCAID

C4D is a building of two halves, split horizontally just below the eaves. The lower half is a rationally planned box centred on a teaching space that allows an uninterrupted view of the nearby airfield; it is supported by a series of meeting rooms, offices and storage areas with simple timber cladding and simple details. The top half could not be more different: its complex juxtaposition of beams and roof planes is unquestionably aeronautical, and it appears to be part biplane and part aircraft hangar. The form is justified by the provision of north light, but is undoubtedly fuelled by imagination. Every joint is an exploration of diagonal geometry in both plan and section, and – given the right conditions – the structure might easily fly.

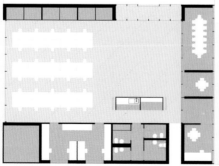

Floor plan

Section

MARSHLAND DISCOVERY ZONE, RSPB RAINHAM MARSHES
PURFLEET, ESSEX

PETER BEARD_LANDROOM

CLIENT: THE ROYAL SOCIETY FOR THE PROTECTION OF BIRDS
STRUCTURAL ENGINEER: JANE WERNICK ASSOCIATES
CONTRACTOR: KIND AND COMPANY (BUILDERS)
CONTRACT VALUE: £600,000
DATE OF COMPLETION: MARCH 2009
GROSS INTERNAL AREA: 83 SQ. M
IMAGES: SUE BARR – VIEW
LONGLISTED FOR THE RIBA STIRLING PRIZE AND SHORTLISTED FOR THE
     STEPHEN LAWRENCE PRIZE
THE ROYAL SOCIETY FOR THE PROTECTION OF BIRDS WAS SHORTLISTED
     FOR THE RIBA CLIENT OF THE YEAR

Three rusty old sea containers dumped on a marsh would not normally be perceived as having any aesthetic or practical value. Still less might they be thought capable of forming a place for exploration and delight. But the rawness inherent in these Cor-ten containers allows them to retain their industrial identity even as they are reinvented as places for observation and learning. Minor modifications have been cleverly made to maintain an ambiguity that is entirely appropriate to the activity and setting. This project is concerned not with the traditional architectural skills of managing form and materials, but with revaluing things that appear no longer to have any use, and encouraging others to do likewise.

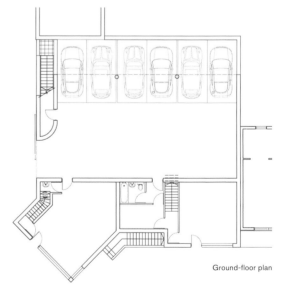

NEWHALL PRIVATE HOUSING
HARLOW

RICHARD MURPHY ARCHITECTS; STUDIO REAL

CLIENT: NEWHALL PROJECTS
STRUCTURAL ENGINEERS: SKM ANTHONY HUNT; WATERMAN STRUCTURES
SERVICES ENGINEER: FULCRUM CONSULTING
CONTRACTOR: VERRY CONSTRUCTION
CONTRACT VALUE: £9,200,000
DATE OF COMPLETION: JANUARY 2011
GROSS INTERNAL AREA: 7241 SQ. M
IMAGES: RICHARD MURPHY ARCHITECTS

There is an optimism at Newhall that attempts to create communities that look beyond the ubiquitous schemes of 'executive homes' surrounded by suburban gardens and a car to mark each front door. The masterplan by Studio Real places housing generally at right angles to the roads, creating walled lanes. Richard Murphy Architects has built on this idea using largely single-aspect houses, the blind back wall of each helping to form the enclosure for a private walled garden for its neighbour. This allows the garden to have a direct relationship with the living area without being overlooked, and to retain a feeling of space. This is precisely the sort of thinking that should be encouraged from housing developers.

Ground-floor plan

RECEPTION HIDE COMPLEX, TITCHWELL MARSH

TITCHWELL, NORFOLK

HAYSOM WARD MILLER ARCHITECTS

CLIENT: THE ROYAL SOCIETY FOR THE PROTECTION OF BIRDS
STRUCTURAL ENGINEER: CAMBRIDGE ARCHITECTURAL RESEARCH
CONTRACTOR: R.G. CARTER
CONTRACT VALUE: £314,000
DATE OF COMPLETION: DECEMBER 2010
GROSS INTERNAL AREA: 164 SQ. M
IMAGES: HAYSOM WARD MILLER ARCHITECTS (BOTTOM); MIKE PAGE (TOP)
THE ROYAL SOCIETY FOR THE PROTECTION OF BIRDS WAS SHORTLISTED
    FOR THE RIBA CLIENT OF THE YEAR

A series of unheated and unserviced timber structures sits astride a raw concrete barrier that provides some defence from floods and creates two very different habitats: a freshwater lagoon and a saltwater marsh. This is a most unusual hide for birdwatching. Rather than a single building, it is a series of special places: a covered area looking along the flood defence and two wing-shaped enclosures, one overlooking fresh water, the other salt. On such a unique site it would have been easy for the architect to get carried away with either elaborate structures or forced minimalism; but the hide does neither, simply saying what it needs to in a gentle, relaxed way.

Site plan

UK CENTRE FOR CARNIVAL ARTS
ST MARY'S ROAD, LUTON

ASH SAKULA ARCHITECTS

CLIENT: UK CENTRE FOR CARNIVAL ARTS
STRUCTURAL ENGINEER: ADAMS KARA TAYLOR
SERVICES ENGINEER: MICHAEL POPPER ASSOCIATES
CONTRACTOR: APOLLO PROPERTY SERVICES GROUP
CONTRACT VALUE: £3,900,000
DATE OF COMPLETION: MARCH 2009
GROSS INTERNAL AREA: 1420 SQ. M
IMAGES: PAUL RIDDLE – VIEW

This is a bold attempt to re-create the feel of an arts community that has developed in an ad hoc way over time. The plan – a group of buildings focused on a yard – is straightforward, and the antithesis of the arts centre itself. Each building has a different character in both form and expression, and, while there is some consistency in the use of materials, there is a clever mismatch in how they are expressed, creating the feeling of using what was to hand. This loose-fit detailing allows the spaces to be inhabited in a relaxed yet creative way that is entirely appropriate to the spirit of Carnival.

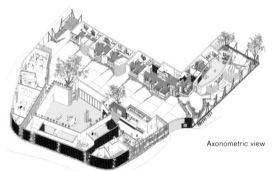

Axonometric view

BIDEFORD COLLEGE
ABBOTSHAM ROAD, BIDEFORD

NPS SOUTH WEST

CLIENT: DEVON COUNTY COUNCIL
STRUCTURAL ENGINEER: PARSONS BRINCKERHOFF
SERVICES ENGINEER: NPS GROUP
CONTRACTOR: MORGAN SINDALL
CONTRACT VALUE: £45,000,000
DATE OF COMPLETION: AUGUST 2010
GROSS INTERNAL AREA: 17,690 SQ. M
IMAGES: GIRTS GAILANS

The college is on a steeply sloping site and has a clear and
legible plan that responds to a complicated and detailed brief.
Classroom wings are arranged in six parallel blocks alongside the
main building, which is an indoor/outdoor space with dining hall
and winter garden. This works well: there are secluded spaces in
which the students can congregate and a long, open space for
assembly. Between each individually coloured classroom block
is an open space, on to which the ground-floor classrooms open.
This once-in-a-lifetime building for Bideford is inherently and
straightforwardly sustainable, and is rated BREEAM 'Excellent'.

Elevation

BROWN'S DENTAL PRACTICE
FORE STREET, IVYBRIDGE

DAVID SHEPPARD ARCHITECTS

CLIENTS: LORNA AND DEREK BROWN
STRUCTURAL ENGINEER: STRUCTURAL SOLUTIONS
QUANTITY SURVEYOR: HART & HUNNAM
CONTRACTOR: SHERWELL VALLEY BUILDERS
CONTRACT VALUE: £524,000
DATE OF COMPLETION: NOVEMBER 2010
GROSS INTERNAL AREA: 304 SQ. M
IMAGES: JOAKIM BOREN
SHORTLISTED FOR THE STEPHEN LAWRENCE PRIZE

This is a feast for the senses, from the overt tactility of the rough-
hewn stone walling to the scent and smooth warmth of the birch
plywood that lines the interior. The quality of light in the treatment
rooms is particularly poetic, with frameless glass rooflights
capturing the dappled light that falls through the surrounding trees.
The architect has worked hard to balance the patients' requirement
for privacy with the practitioners' need for an airy, light-filled
workspace. The narrow slots between the planks of cedar cladding
are glazed, giving patients glimpses outside. Such delight in
material and texture is a welcome contrast to the functionality
and lack of care so often associated with healthcare buildings.

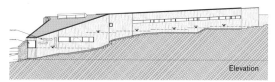

Elevation

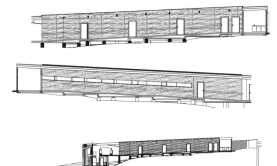

Sections

WEST BUCKLAND SCHOOL
WEST BUCKLAND, BARNSTAPLE

MRJ RUNDELL + ASSOCIATES

CLIENT: WEST BUCKLAND SCHOOL
STRUCTURAL ENGINEER: ATELIER ONE
SERVICES ENGINEER: E3 CONSULTING ENGINEERS
CONTRACTOR: PEARCE CONSTRUCTION (BARNSTAPLE)
CONTRACT VALUE: £3,250,000
DATE OF COMPLETION: MARCH 2010
GROSS INTERNAL AREA: 1400 SQ. M
IMAGES: DANIEL BURT (TOP); PAUL MCCARTHY (BOTTOM)

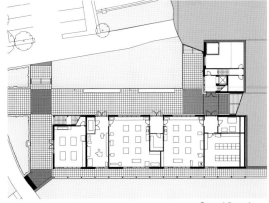

Ground-floor plan

Here is a work of architecture that generates aesthetic and social stimuli in support of a wider cultural agenda, and demonstrates what the perfect environment for teaching art might be like. This wonderfully clear and confident addition to a Victorian school is divided into two simple linear buildings, one a studio theatre that aligns with the original buildings, the other a rigorous extrusion of workshops and studios. A new public court at the eastern end serves as a performance area. Subtle shifts in section, using half levels across the sloping site, allow a glazed bridge to connect the elements. It feels like an unpretentious but supportive place in which to be creative.

Section

BOURNE HILL OFFICES
BOURNE HILL, SALISBURY

STANTON WILLIAMS

CLIENT: WILTSHIRE COUNCIL
STRUCTURAL ENGINEER: ADAMS KARA TAYLOR
SERVICES ENGINEER: MAX FORDHAM
CONTRACTOR: MORGAN SINDALL
CONTRACT VALUE: £15,800,000
DATE OF COMPLETION: AUGUST 2010
GROSS INTERNAL AREA: 4147 SQ. M
IMAGES: HUFTON & CROW – VIEW

This project involved the creation of new public gardens, the restoration and repair of an existing building and, wonderfully, the clearing away of car parking from the latter's front entrance, producing a new civic space for Salisbury. The new work is architecturally bold enough to compete gently with the existing structure in a manner that enhances the qualities of both new and old. Materials and construction are meticulously considered: most evident are the tactile stone-clad free-standing columns, which act as fins to shade the seamless glazed façade, producing a single elegant planar surface and an unexpected and dramatic impression of scale. Although it accommodates largely private, back-office functions, this is a truly civic building.

CIRCLEBATH

FOXCOTE AVENUE, PEASEDOWN ST JOHN, BATH

FOSTER + PARTNERS

CLIENTS: CIRCLE; HEALTH PROPERTIES MANAGEMENT
STRUCTURAL ENGINEER: WSP CANTOR SEINUK
SERVICES ENGINEER: ARUP
CONTRACTOR: VINCI CONSTRUCTION UK
CONTRACT VALUE: CONFIDENTIAL
DATE OF COMPLETION: OCTOBER 2009
GROSS INTERNAL AREA: 6367 SQ. M
IMAGES: CIRCLE (BOTTOM); NIGEL YOUNG – FOSTER + PARTNERS (TOP)
LONGLISTED FOR THE RIBA STIRLING PRIZE

CircleBath aspires to transform radically the way in which health buildings are designed and healthcare provided. The strategy of drawing on expertise from other fields – such as the hospitality and airport sectors – while testing and challenging the norms and regulations governing hospital design has produced a highly intelligent yet straightforward building. The abundance and quality of light and its interplay with materials, textures and colours create an environment that is simultaneously confident, luxurious, uplifting, soothing and calm. All this produces a clear message that the patient is in safe hands. The clarity of the plan and the simplicity of the section create an intuitive circulation, making the building easy to navigate and obviating much of the need for signage or maps.

First-floor plan

MAGGIE'S CHELTENHAM

THE LODGE, CHELTENHAM GENERAL HOSPITAL, COLLEGE BATHS ROAD, CHELTENHAM

MJP ARCHITECTS

CLIENT: MAGGIE'S CENTRES
STRUCTURAL ENGINEER: PRICE & MYERS
M&E ENGINEER: K.J. TAIT ENGINEERS
MAIN CONTRACTOR: DAY BUILDING CONTRACTORS
CONTRACT VALUE: CONFIDENTIAL
DATE OF COMPLETION: AUGUST 2010
GROSS INTERNAL AREA: CONFIDENTIAL
IMAGES: PETER DURANT – ARCAID

This project has been conceived at a micro scale, almost as a piece of cabinet-making rather than a building. It has been designed from the inside out, and the ingenious manipulation of scale has produced an intimate, domestic and very social space. The building is crafted with refinement and sensuously detailed, with edges and junctions meticulously expressed. Colour, material and light are used to great effect, creating an environment that is robust and tactile, jewel-like and rich. The use of mirrors and visual illusions is both appropriate and refreshing. The building unfolds to reveal internal views that are complex and multilayered, but views out are cleverly controlled to edit a somewhat messy site.

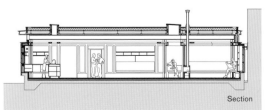

Section

PARABOLA ARTS CENTRE, THE CHELTENHAM LADIES' COLLEGE

PARABOLA ROAD, CHELTENHAM

FOSTER WILSON ARCHITECTS

CLIENT: THE CHELTENHAM LADIES' COLLEGE
STRUCTURAL ENGINEER: PRICE & MYERS
SERVICES ENGINEER: MAX FORDHAM
CONTRACTOR: WILLMOTT DIXON
CONTRACT VALUE: £6,200,000
DATE OF COMPLETION: OCTOBER 2009
GROSS INTERNAL AREA: 2080 SQ. M
IMAGES: JAMES BRITTAIN – VIEW (TOP LEFT AND RIGHT); PHIL HARVEY (BOTTOM)

It is refreshing to see classical language employed with such restraint. The architect had a tough challenge – to extend a detached villa that appeared to be two semi-detached homes – but has used the opportunity of the inherited dual circulation to organize the complex programme of the new building. The scale and simplicity of form are appropriate to the surrounding townscape. The auditorium is intimate but with a degree of gravitas that befits the formal expression of the architecture; it is flexible and comfortable and benefits from natural light, and the technical problems of acoustics, ventilation and other services have been addressed with elegance and care. The building has transformed and cemented the relationship between the college and the town.

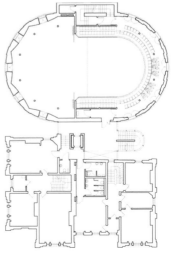

First-floor plan

KENDREW QUADRANGLE, ST JOHN'S COLLEGE

ST GILES, OXFORD

MJP ARCHITECTS

CLIENT: ST JOHN'S COLLEGE
STRUCTURAL ENGINEER: PRICE & MYERS
SERVICES ENGINEER: MICHAEL POPPER ASSOCIATES
CONTRACTOR: KINGERLEE
CONTRACT VALUE: CONFIDENTIAL
DATE OF COMPLETION: SEPTEMBER 2010
GROSS INTERNAL AREA: 6000 SQ. M
IMAGES: PETER DURANT – ARCAID
LONGLISTED FOR THE RIBA STIRLING PRIZE

This project is very comfortable in its setting, a south-facing quadrangle that focuses on a mature beech tree. In its covered cloisters and glazed common-room roofs, in the student rooms and external terraces, it blurs the definition between inside and out. The building is a journey of discovery, with a series of delightfully framed views through architectural spaces on to the garden. The college wanted its new building to reflect the latest thinking in sustainability, and the combination of orientation, excellent insulation, solar and geothermal energy, biomass boilers, heat recovery, low-energy lighting and controls could hardly be bettered. All this has been achieved without the slightest hint of compromise in the architecture.

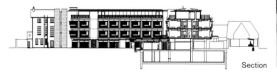

Section

LIFE SCIENCES BUILDING, UNIVERSITY OF SOUTHAMPTON

HIGHFIELD CAMPUS, SOUTHAMPTON

NBBJ

CLIENT: UNIVERSITY OF SOUTHAMPTON
STRUCTURAL ENGINEER: ADAMS KARA TAYLOR
SERVICES ENGINEER: ARUP
CONTRACTOR: BAM CONSTRUCTION UK
CONTRACT VALUE: £35,000,000
DATE OF COMPLETION: AUGUST 2010
GROSS INTERNAL AREA: 10,000 SQ. M
IMAGES: GARY BRITTON (TOP); EDMUND SUMNER – VIEW (CENTRE AND
    BOTTOM)

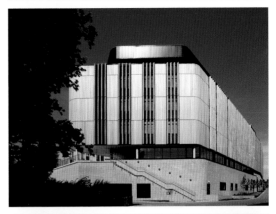

In bringing together students and academics from the schools of Medicine and Biological Sciences, as well as additional research groups from the School of Electronics and Computer Science, the building reflects the university's cross-disciplinary research vision. It is rationally and efficiently laid out, with views across the atrium and into the areas that house the various functions, but it is the irregular spaces between these elements, together with the half levels formed by the taller laboratories, that make the project particularly memorable. Natural ventilation is used where possible, and thermal mass is exposed to create a comfortable working environment. The building is active at every level: well lit, with intriguing perspectives, it works environmentally and – just as importantly – acoustically.

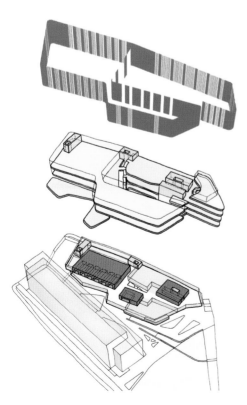

Axonometric view

Elevation

THE ROTHSCHILD FOUNDATION

WINDMILL HILL, SILK STREET, WADDESDON, AYLESBURY

STEPHEN MARSHALL ARCHITECTS

CLIENT: THE ALICE TRUST
STRUCTURAL ENGINEER: THORNTON TOMASETTI
SERVICES ENGINEER: MAX FORDHAM
CONTRACTOR: KINGERLEE
CONTRACT VALUE: £8,000,000
DATE OF COMPLETION: FEBRUARY 2011
GROSS INTERNAL AREA: 1610 SQ. M
IMAGES: RICHARD BRYANT – ARCAID
LONGLISTED FOR THE RIBA STIRLING PRIZE

A series of simple rectangular buildings was built on the site of a former dairy farm, to house the Rothschild Foundation Archive and the charity's offices. The original farmhouse was retained and the outbuildings incorporated into a new composition of courtyard gardens. The main archive is accommodated in a building with great thermal mass and insulation. It is naturally cooled, thus avoiding the need most archives have for air conditioning and forced humidity control. An exquisite oak gridshell roof, consummately detailed and supported on triangular struts, forms the major space. The landscaped courtyards complement the architecture, and the decorated, diagonally incised zinc roofs add richness to the simple architectural forms.

Floor plan

WATSON HOUSE

NEW FOREST NATIONAL PARK

JOHN PARDEY ARCHITECTS

CLIENTS: CHARLES AND FIONA WATSON
STRUCTURAL ENGINEER: RAMBOLL UK
QUANTITY SURVEYOR: APS ASSOCIATES
CONTRACTOR: NFTS CONSTRUCTION (CEASED TRADING) SUCCEEDED BY
    ED RICE
CONTRACT VALUE: £640,000
DATE OF COMPLETION: SEPTEMBER 2010
GROSS INTERNAL AREA: 318 SQ. M
IMAGES: JAMES MORRIS – VIEW
SHORTLISTED FOR THE RIBA MANSER MEDAL

The architect has overcome the restrictions of the planners, who insisted that this New Forest house be invisible from the public realm, in a thoroughly elegant way. Its concept is beautifully simple: a long, linear shape with a central living space that is open at both ends. While it pays homage to mid-century Danish examples, the architecture is enriched by the playful humour of the quirkily placed windows. Structural panels of locally grown sweet chestnut minimized the house's embodied energy and allowed it to be built quickly. It is staked to the ground by its broad brick chimney, but otherwise floats delightfully above the landscape, a poetic structure of a type that is all too rare in the English countryside.

Site plan

DOVER ESPLANADE
WATERLOO CRESCENT, DOVER

TONKIN LIU

CLIENTS: KENT COUNTY COUNCIL; SEA CHANGE (DEPARTMENT FOR
    CULTURE, MEDIA AND SPORT/COMMISSION FOR ARCHITECTURE AND
    THE BUILT ENVIRONMENT); DOVER HARBOUR BOARD; DOVER DISTRICT
    COUNCIL
STRUCTURAL ENGINEER: RODRIGUES ASSOCIATES
CONTRACTOR: RINGWAY INFRASTRUCTURE SERVICES
CONTRACT VALUE: £2,000,000
DATE OF COMPLETION: AUGUST 2010
GROSS INTERNAL AREA: 6000 SQ. M
IMAGES: ROBBIE POLLEY (TOP AND CENTRE); MIKE TONKIN (BOTTOM)

Dover's seafront has been transformed by artworks that take the
form of three waves gently washing against the sheltered beach.
The 'Lifting Wave' is a repeating form of curving white-concrete
ramps and staircases that rise and fall to connect the esplanade
to the beach. The 'Resting Wave' is a second sculptural white-
concrete wall made up of a series of moulded curves; its recesses
house oak benches, its promontories raised lawns. Third is the
'Lighting Wave', with lighting columns that rise and fall like froth
on the crest of a wave. These deceptively effortless interventions
lend this shoreline path a true sense of place and fun.

HOUSE IN EPSOM

THE RIDGE, EPSOM

ELDRIDGE SMERIN

CLIENTS: IAN AND LELYANA HARRIS
STRUCTURAL ENGINEER: TALL CONSULTING STRUCTURAL ENGINEERS
SERVICES ENGINEER: STUDIO NINE ENVIRONMENTAL ENGINEERING
    CONSULTANTS
CONTRACTORS: ROBIN ELLIS PROJECTS; TORIC CONSTRUCTION MANAGEMENT
CONTRACT VALUE: £2,600,000
DATE OF COMPLETION: JANUARY 2010
GROSS INTERNAL AREA: 715 SQ. M
IMAGES: LYNDON DOUGLAS
SHORTLISTED FOR THE RIBA MANSER MEDAL

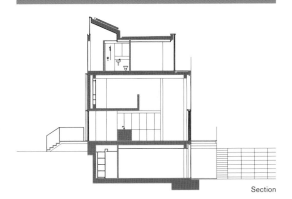

Section

Externally, this is a modern and uncompromising work of contemporary architecture. But the massing and unrelenting geometry hide a delightfully homely, warm and welcoming interior. The concept is strong, with equilateral triangles throughout the plan: the house is angled at 60 degrees to the pool wing, while the columns and the garden planters are also triangular, the former in section and the latter in plan. Rather wonderfully, the house displays a touch of the obsessiveness of Frank Lloyd Wright. It ticks all the right environmental boxes, too: seven 80-metre-deep boreholes for ground-source heating, solar thermal water-heating panels, concrete as a heat store and windows that open. The pure and relentless architecture is enjoyable because the house is, above all, a lovely home.

MISSION HALL
RICKMAN'S LANE, PLAISTOW, WEST SUSSEX

ADAM RICHARDS ARCHITECTS

CLIENTS: NICHOLAS TAYLOR AND DEAN WHEELER
STRUCTURAL ENGINEER: STRUCTURE WORKSHOP
CONTRACTOR: CEECOM
CONTRACT VALUE: CONFIDENTIAL
DATE OF COMPLETION: OCTOBER 2010
GROSS INTERNAL AREA: 150 SQ. M
IMAGES: ADAM RICHARDS
SHORTLISTED FOR THE RIBA MANSER MEDAL

This small house sits on a bend in the road on the site of a former Baptist chapel, between a large oak and a drovers' way, with long Sussex views to the west. Two slim offset buildings are joined by an entrance reached via a staircase. The interior is a delight. Downstairs, solid and secure, cave-like black stone forms niches, with white-brick barrel-vaulted ceilings and lots of oak cupboards. Upstairs, airy and light, irregular oak floorboards give way to full-height 4-metre windows in deep reveals – a diminutive *piano nobile*. This is beautiful design on a small, difficult site, an accomplished and unique piece of architecture that is simultaneously complex and simple, as are all the very best things in life.

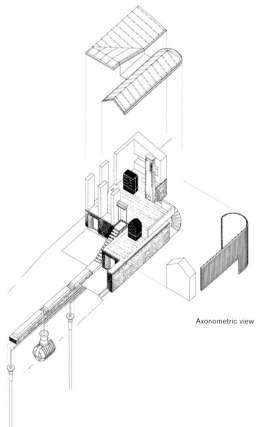

Axonometric view

Section

NO. 1 SMITHERY

THE HISTORIC DOCKYARD, CHATHAM

VAN HEYNINGEN AND HAWARD ARCHITECTS

CLIENTS: CHATHAM HISTORIC DOCKYARD TRUST; IMPERIAL WAR MUSEUM;
    NATIONAL MARITIME MUSEUM
STRUCTURAL ENGINEER: PRICE & MYERS
SERVICES ENGINEER: MAX FORDHAM
CONTRACTORS: KINGSWOOD CONSTRUCTION (EMERGENCY STABILIZATION
    WORKS); R.J. BARWICK, ISG (MAIN WORKS)
CONTRACT VALUE: £9,500,000
DATE OF COMPLETION: JULY 2010
GROSS INTERNAL AREA: 4445 SQ. M
IMAGES: JAMES BRITTAIN – VIEW
CHATHAM HISTORIC DOCKYARD TRUST WAS SHORTLISTED FOR THE RIBA
    CLIENT OF THE YEAR

This is a museum within a museum; its function is to show both its
own structure and the objects it houses. The existing buildings –
falling down but still majestic – have been artfully retained and
gently restored. The new exhibition spaces are rendered abstract
boxes, constructed as separate elements, that sit quietly in the
stately Georgian sheds. Highly insulated, air-tight and with
thermal mass, they require very little beyond minimal temperature
control and low lighting. They provide a sophisticated, controlled
twenty-first-century museum environment, and so can operate
successfully within the conserved historic fabric. Once inside
them you are in a space that has no presence but is simply
dedicated to the display of the exhibits. The contrast between
the old and new spaces is stark and telling.

SHINGLE HOUSE
DUNGENESS ROAD, DUNGENESS

NORD

CLIENT: LIVING ARCHITECTURE
STRUCTURAL ENGINEER: JANE WERNICK ASSOCIATES
SERVICES ENGINEER: ZEF CONCEPTS
CONTRACTOR: ECOLIBRIUM SOLUTIONS
CONTRACT VALUE: CONFIDENTIAL
DATE OF COMPLETION: CONFIDENTIAL
GROSS INTERNAL AREA: CONFIDENTIAL
IMAGES: CHARLES HOSEA

This house, built for hire under the Living Architecture scheme, lends itself to poetic description. Its engagement with the unique landscape of Dungeness is total, and it sits on the shingle desert like a sculpted piece of burnt driftwood. The house merges the mystical and the vernacular, with blackened timber façades, white wainscoted interior and polished-concrete hearth. Then there are the hidden gems: the secret sliding doors, the air-source heat pumps, heat recovery in the external walls, no gutters (the rain runs off into the shingle, which is said to be nearly 5 kilometres deep). As soon as you enter you get a sense of comfort and calm belonging, and it is hard to imagine feeling like a guest here for long. It is a beautiful and accomplished study in architecture.

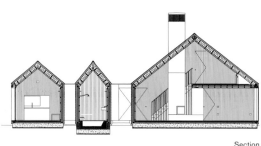

Section

THE SPACE, SEVENOAKS SCHOOL
HIGH STREET, SEVENOAKS

TIM RONALDS ARCHITECTS

CLIENT: SEVENOAKS SCHOOL FOUNDATION
STRUCTURAL ENGINEER: PRICE & MYERS
SERVICES ENGINEER: MAX FORDHAM
CONTRACTOR: R. DURTNELL & SONS
CONTRACT VALUE: £8,800,000
DATE OF COMPLETION: APRIL 2010
GROSS INTERNAL AREA: 3450 SQ. M
IMAGES: DAVID MEREWETHER (BOTTOM); CHRISTIAN RICHTERS – VIEW (TOP)
LONGLISTED FOR THE RIBA STIRLING PRIZE

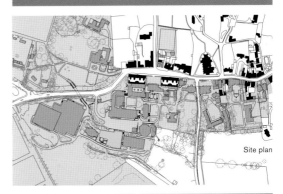

Site plan

This is the real thing: architecture that sings. Fluid, artfully modelled spaces have been crafted and detailed with care, and are of high quality. From public performance spaces to intimate practice rooms, all are related to one another but perfectly fulfil their own functions. The view from the foyer takes in the two-storey fall across the site as the staircase leads you down to the open, glazed recital room and the Arcadian scene beyond. The concert hall is a beautiful daylit barn of a space, warm and majestic with a towering Douglas fir-boarded ceiling, cranked timber-and-steel trusses sitting on solid brick walls, and concrete columns. The acoustics derive from the geometry rather than being created artificially. The teaching block marks a total change in scale, its rooms functional cells, daylit and finely tuned.

BARKING CENTRAL
BARKING

ALLFORD HALL MONAGHAN MORRIS; MUF

CLIENTS: REDROW REGENERATION (BARKING); LONDON BOROUGH OF
    BARKING & DAGENHAM
STRUCTURAL ENGINEERS: BURO HAPPOLD (PHASE ONE); BEATTIE
    WATKINSON PARTNERS (PHASE TWO)
SERVICES ENGINEERS: FABER MAUNSELL, KIER, CPC MECHANICAL &
    ELECTRICAL SERVICES (PHASE ONE); ATELIER TEN, CPC MECHANICAL &
    ELECTRICAL SERVICES (PHASE TWO)
CONTRACTOR: ARDMORE CONSTRUCTION
CONTRACT VALUE: £72,000,000
DATE OF COMPLETION: JUNE 2007 (PHASE ONE); NOVEMBER 2008 (PHASE TWO)
GROSS INTERNAL AREA: 44,050 SQ. M
IMAGES: TIMOTHY SOAR

In 1999 the London Borough of Barking & Dagenham set
the architects a tough challenge: to regenerate Barking town
centre predominantly with housing. The development has been
accomplished with great wit, energy and a certain aplomb. The
scheme, which was realized in two phases, consisted of seven
new buildings and the reinvention of a drab 1970s library into
a modern learning centre; retail space; a hotel; 500 flats; and,
critically, extensive public-realm works carried out in collaboration
with the architecture firm Muf. Each building takes on a different
persona through the exuberant use of material shifts, colour and
texture. The architects have adopted a bold and graphically
articulated tower – the seventeen-storey Lemonade Building – as
a key signal of change visible to a wider area.

Section

BEAR LANE
GREAT SUFFOLK STREET, SE1

PANTER HUDSPITH ARCHITECTS

CLIENT: GALLIARD HOMES
STRUCTURAL ENGINEER: CLARK SMITH PARTNERSHIP
SERVICES ENGINEER: CSA CONSULTING ENGINEERS
CONTRACTOR: GALLIARD CONSTRUCTION
CONTRACT VALUE: £12,000,000
DATE OF COMPLETION: MAY 2009
GROSS INTERNAL AREA: 8828 SQ. M
IMAGES: KEITH COLLIE (CENTRE); PANTER HUDSPITH ARCHITECTS (TOP; BOTTOM)
LONGLISTED FOR THE RIBA STIRLING PRIZE

Bear Lane so clearly and substantially elevates itself above the benchmark of standard urban housing design that it is surprising to discover it is the result of a volume house builder operating through a design-and-build contract. A terrace of tall individual brick buildings is understood as both a series of elements and a singular entity, with a crenellated skyline and heavily articulated façades. The project wraps a triangular site, rising from a retained corner pub that historically and formally anchors the scheme. Three façades look into a communal courtyard. This is sophisticated residential architecture of the highest order.

Site plan

163

CHELSEA ACADEMY
LOTS ROAD, SW10

FEILDEN CLEGG BRADLEY STUDIOS

CLIENTS: DEPARTMENT FOR EDUCATION; CHELSEA ACADEMY TRUST
STRUCTURAL ENGINEER: PRICE & MYERS
SERVICES ENGINEER: FULCRUM CONSULTING
CONTRACTOR: WATES CONSTRUCTION
CONTRACT VALUE: £34,600,000
DATE OF COMPLETION: SEPTEMBER 2010
GROSS INTERNAL AREA: 11,000 SQ. M
IMAGES: TIM CROCKER
LONGLISTED FOR THE RIBA STIRLING PRIZE

The building packs 11,000 square metres of school into a highly constrained site exactly half that size. The quality of the circulation and teaching spaces is the result of a highly sophisticated synthesis of complex requirements. The school sits cheek by jowl with low-rise housing and a power station, and makes sense of the spaces in between in a neighbourly way. It steps between the two through a series of courtyards that bring in light and provide external space. The building's layout, section and form are a remarkable three-dimensional puzzle in the manner of a Rubik's cube, with each face having an independent response to its immediate environment. The design team has developed advanced environmental controls to integrate passive design with technology and to reduce carbon emissions by 10 per cent.

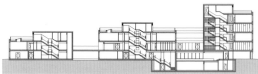

Section

CHISWICK HOUSE CAFE
BURLINGTON LANE, W4

CARUSO ST JOHN ARCHITECTS

CLIENT: CHISWICK HOUSE & GARDENS TRUST
STRUCTURAL ENGINEER: GIFFORD
SERVICES ENGINEER: ROGER PARKER ASSOCIATES
CONTRACTOR: THOMAS SINDEN
CONTRACT VALUE: £1,300,000
DATE OF COMPLETION: FEBRUARY 2010
GROSS INTERNAL AREA: 356 SQ. M
IMAGES: HÉLÈNE BINET

White and pristine in the landscape, with a perimeter arcade and a flat roofline, the Chiswick House Cafe is a worthy addition to William Kent's eighteenth-century landscape. For a modest building this pavilion has great scale, stature, solidity and permanence. The external colonnade is formed of tall, load-bearing columns made of beautiful white Portland stone with the texture of travertine. But the building is not symmetrical in plan; rather, it is L-shaped, with the perimeter arcade angled almost imperceptibly and the openings between the columns not aligned with the windows. As a result, from the inside the building feels more enclosed. These adaptations to the geometry are carried out with an assured hand, and have captured the classical essence of the Palladian Chiswick House in a completely new way.

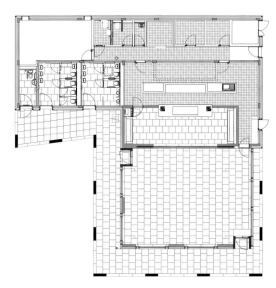

Floor plan

CITY OF WESTMINSTER COLLEGE
PADDINGTON GREEN CAMPUS, W2

SCHMIDT HAMMER LASSEN ARCHITECTS

CLIENT: CITY OF WESTMINSTER COLLEGE
STRUCTURAL ENGINEER: BURO HAPPOLD
CONTRACTOR: MCLAREN CONSTRUCTION GROUP
CONTRACT VALUE: £67,700,000
DATE OF COMPLETION: JANUARY 2011
GROSS INTERNAL AREA: 24,000 SQ. M
IMAGES: ADAM MØRK
LONGLISTED FOR THE RIBA STIRLING PRIZE

This new flagship campus for the City of Westminster College
consolidates accommodation from several sites in one building.
Remarkably, given its location, scale, footprint and height (seven
storeys), it achieves great composure and provides a light, calm
and welcoming environment. At first glance, to passing traffic on
the nearby Westway, the college is akin to an ocean liner, with
strong horizontal lines between which glazing and blue vertical
panels create a subdued watery shimmer. Entrance is through
a wide central atrium, lit by an ETFE roof, with a main staircase
that doubles as seating for assemblies. The materials palette
throughout is sparse and cool, with *in-situ* concrete columns and
soffits, stone flooring and pale timber mullions and wall finishes.

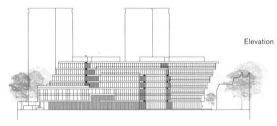

Elevation

CLAREDALE STREET
CLAREDALE STREET AND MANSFORD STREET, E2

KARAKUSEVIC CARSON ARCHITECTS

CLIENT: TOWER HAMLETS COMMUNITY HOUSING
STRUCTURAL/SERVICES ENGINEER: ATELIER TEN
CONTRACTOR: HILL PARTNERSHIPS
CONTRACT VALUE: £10,000,000
DATE OF COMPLETION: MAY 2010
GROSS INTERNAL AREA: 51,000 SQ. M
IMAGES: TIM CROCKER

Prior to the tower blocks of the 1960s and 1970s – at their best typified by Denys Lasdun's Keeling House, now a feted and gated cluster of private flats – this area was characterized by Victorian terraces. It is that typology and scale that the architect has reintroduced, creating eminently liveable places. The old street pattern is re-established.

The architect has considered carefully issues of public and private space, creating active frontages to streets, shared courtyards and private gardens. The architectural treatment is thoroughly contemporary, with copper to raise the material sense of the project across all types of tenure. The overall sense is one of modesty, intelligence and sensitivity to people and how they might live their lives.

Section

FITZROY STREET AND MAPLE PLACE
W1

DUGGAN MORRIS ARCHITECTS

CLIENT: DERWENT LONDON
STRUCTURAL ENGINEER: AKERA ENGINEERS
CONTRACTOR: THE THORNTON PARTNERSHIP
CONTRACT VALUE: £2,500,000
DATE OF COMPLETION: NOVEMBER 2010
GROSS INTERNAL AREA: 2400 SQ. M
IMAGES: KILIAN O'SULLIVAN – VIEW

Duggan Morris has carefully modified a couple of existing office buildings to create two conjoined but separately lettable spaces that have similar characters but are also different from each other. In carrying out the refurbishment, the architect retained as much of the existing fabric as possible, so that the interventions are simple yet elemental. The apparent simplicity belies the fact that this was a complex refurbishment. The clarity of the spaces and the sheer elegance of the inserted elements – red-brown balustrading, light fittings and way-finding against white backgrounds – are the result of an almost obsessive attention to detail. There are no irrelevant flourishes. Every design move is proportionate and deliberate, and embodies the pared-down character of the building.

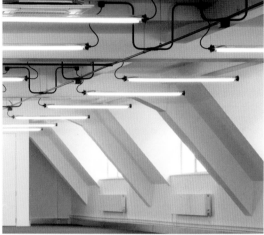

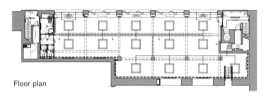

Floor plan

H10 HOTEL
WATERLOO ROAD, SE1

MACCREANOR LAVINGTON

CLIENT: H10 HOTELS
STRUCTURAL ENGINEER: HALCROW YOLLES
SERVICES ENGINEER: FREEMAN BEESLEY
CONTRACTOR: GALLIFORD TRY
CONTRACT VALUE: £14,500,000
DATE OF COMPLETION: DECEMBER 2009
GROSS INTERNAL AREA: 15,000 SQ. M
IMAGES: TIM CROCKER (CENTRE; BOTTOM); HUFTON & CROW – VIEW (TOP)

Troubled histories almost always show in the fabric of buildings, but Maccreanor Lavington's landmark four-star Waterloo hotel shows little sign of having started out at the planning stage as a housing development. Given the huge constraints imposed by the junction site, that creative flexibility is all the more remarkable. The narrowness of the plot has produced a striking civic composition, clearly defining the base, middle and top of the building. A ground-level cut-back provides a generous pedestrian route, enlivening the street frontage and creating an overhang that shelters the glazed entrance foyer. This is a mature exercise in taming a large façade.

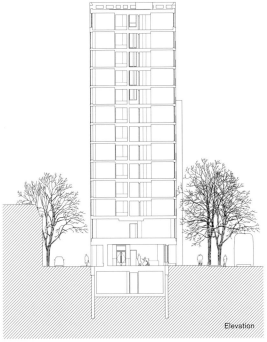

Elevation

HACKNEY SERVICE CENTRE
HILLMAN STREET, E8

HOPKINS ARCHITECTS

CLIENT: LONDON BOROUGH OF HACKNEY
STRUCTURAL ENGINEER: HALCROW GROUP
SERVICES ENGINEER: JACOBS UK
CONTRACT VALUE: £43,732,962
DATE OF COMPLETION: MARCH 2010
GROSS INTERNAL AREA: 15,000 SQ. M
IMAGES: PAUL TYAGI
LONDON BOROUGH OF HACKNEY WAS SHORTLISTED FOR THE RIBA CLIENT
    OF THE YEAR

This significant project brings together under one roof the
services of the London Borough of Hackney. The architectural
proposition is disarmingly straightforward. A U-shaped stacked
plan of administrative space, five storeys high, opens on to a
huge barrel-vaulted glazed atrium. Each of the office floor plates
is predominantly open-plan, with side wings that contain support
spaces, informal meeting and break-out areas, and tea points.

The ground floor of the atrium houses the 'one-stop shop'
for council services, and acts as the interface between the
public and its civil servants. The staff can see the public, and,
importantly, the public can see the staff; this is a project that is
based on the idea of visibility and accessibility. The entire
building is drenched in daylight – the antithesis of a closed,
defensive civic headquarters.

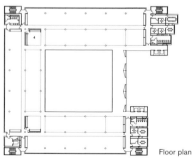

Floor plan

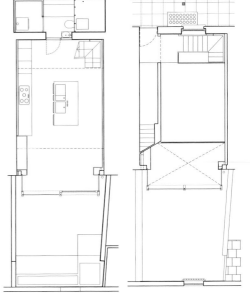

HOXTON HOUSE
BUTTESLAND STREET, N1

DAVID MIKHAIL ARCHITECTS

CLIENT: PRIVATE
STRUCTURAL ENGINEER: BTA STRUCTURAL DESIGN
CONTRACTOR: EURO BUILD CONTRACTORS
CONTRACT VALUE: £200,000
DATE OF COMPLETION: JULY 2010
GROSS INTERNAL AREA: 124 SQ. M
IMAGES: TIM CROCKER
SHORTLISTED FOR THE STEPHEN LAWRENCE PRIZE

Britain has an enormous stock of traditional terraced houses, yet they increasingly struggle to meet the needs of contemporary living. This typical four-storey London terraced house is a case in point, characterized by multiple levels and cramped, dark rooms set around a winding staircase. The clue to realizing its full potential was in the small rear garden. The lower-ground and ground floors have been unified by the addition of a modest double-height glass extension, just 1 metre deep. This has allowed both storeys to be pulled away from the existing rear wall, achieving a delightful sense of space and light that is hard to believe possible in a house of this type.

Lower-ground-floor plan

Ground-floor plan

KILBURN GRANGE PARK ADVENTURE PLAYGROUND
KILBURN GRANGE PARK, NW6

ERECT ARCHITECTURE

CLIENT: LONDON BOROUGH OF CAMDEN
STRUCTURAL ENGINEER: TALL CONSULTING STRUCTURAL ENGINEERS
CONTRACTOR: KIER WALLIS
CONTRACT VALUE: £976,000
DATE OF COMPLETION: MAY 2010
GROSS INTERNAL AREA: 4032 SQ. M
IMAGES: DAVID GRANDORGE

In an increasingly risk-averse culture, what distinguishes this project is its ambition to challenge and rethink the health-and-safety preconceptions that surround children's playgrounds, most obviously characterized by the ubiquitous use of 'bouncy tarmac'. Instead of approaching the project from a standpoint of risk aversion, architect and client have adopted one of risk benefit, whereby the learning benefits to children during supervised play of encountering reasonable degrees of risk – including fire and water – outweigh the potential dangers.

Within the adventure playground is a whimsical timber play centre that in many ways resembles a big piece of playground furniture. This imaginative thinking has produced a visually, physically and educationally stimulating series of play structures that are characterized by their extensive use of reclaimed and recycled materials.

Elevation

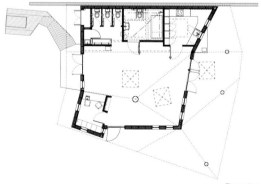

Floor plan

LEIGHTON HOUSE MUSEUM
HOLLAND PARK ROAD, W14

PURCELL MILLER TRITTON

CLIENT: ROYAL BOROUGH OF KENSINGTON AND CHELSEA
STRUCTURAL ENGINEER: MORTON PARTNERSHIP
SERVICES ENGINEER: HARLEY HADDOW
CONTRACTOR: CONISTON
CONTRACT VALUE: CONFIDENTIAL
DATE OF COMPLETION: APRIL 2010
IMAGES: WILL PRYCE – ARCAID

The centrepiece of Leighton House, designed in 1864 to display
Lord Leighton's collection of Islamic tiles, is the opulent two-storey
domed Arab Hall with a central fountain. The whole interior of the
house is richly decorated, with ceramic tiles, rich paintwork and
gilded ceilings. The building had subsequently been extended
and used as a school. For its restoration, the architect removed
much of the troubling ephemera that had accumulated over the
years, and paid meticulous attention to services, redecoration,
lighting and complex external reinstatements, including the
restoration of the rooftop ziggurat. Thanks to painstaking research,
a strong collaboration between client and architect, and a careful
eking out of the budget, the original character of the building has
been accurately, although not slavishly, re-created. This is a
masterpiece of conservation.

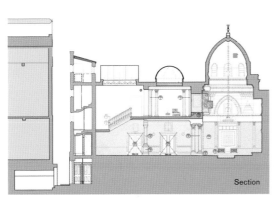

Section

Elevation

MICHAEL FARADAY SCHOOL
PORTLAND STREET, SE17

ARCHIAL ARCHITECTS

CLIENT: LONDON BOROUGH OF SOUTHWARK, CHILDREN'S SERVICES
STRUCTURAL/SERVICES ENGINEER: BURO HAPPOLD
CONTRACTOR: GALLIFORD TRY
CONTRACT VALUE: £8,842,053
DATE OF COMPLETION: SEPTEMBER 2010
GROSS INTERNAL AREA: 3021 SQ. M
IMAGES: MORLEY VON STERNBERG – ARCAID

This primary school's cheerful demeanour is a natural counter-reaction to its context – the bleak slabs of the Aylesbury Estate – but it poses two questions: does the building have substance as well as style, and does the child-friendly form alienate the adult learners who also use the site? In fact, behind the various plays of colour and form is a well-planned and serious school.

The main building is a drum, with adult learning occupying a two-storey segment facing the street. Children enter on the opposite side into two storeys of classrooms set in a horseshoe arrangement around an atrium. This organization makes for a vibrant and interactive school environment. The drum is topped by a sophisticated roof composed of a deep glulam grid with pitched rooflights and acoustic baffles.

NEW HERBARIUM, LIBRARY, ART AND ARCHIVES WING
ROYAL BOTANIC GARDENS, KEW

EDWARD CULLINAN ARCHITECTS

CLIENT: ROYAL BOTANIC GARDENS, KEW
STRUCTURAL ENGINEER: BURO HAPPOLD
CONTRACTOR: WILLMOTT DIXON
CONTRACT VALUE: £16,000,000
DATE OF COMPLETION: JUNE 2009
GROSS INTERNAL AREA: 5000 SQ. M
IMAGES: TIMOTHY SOAR

The new wing to the Herbarium of 1853 provides a modern storage facility for the most vulnerable items in the existing collection of 7 million plant specimens and manuscripts. The plan is essentially that of a three-storey rectangular red-brick storage vault, linked to the main building by a cylindrical three-storey structure, clad in western red cedar and glass, that also houses the reception, the library and a circular reading room. The buildings are arranged to create a new entrance courtyard to the side of the main building. The new storage areas are designed to keep the collection at a constant temperature of 15°C, and use mechanical air-handling and ground-source heat pumps to reduce CO_2 emissions. The building has a BREEAM 'Excellent' rating.

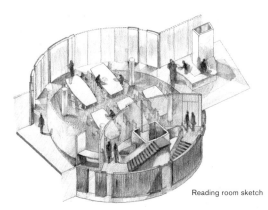

Reading room sketch

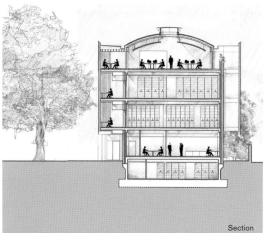

Section

ONE NEW CHANGE
NEW CHANGE, EC4

**ATELIERS JEAN NOUVEL WITH
SIDELL GIBSON ARCHITECTS**

CLIENT: LAND SECURITIES
STRUCTURAL ENGINEER: ARUP
SERVICES ENGINEER: HOARE LEA
CONTRACTOR: BOVIS LEND LEASE
CONTRACT VALUE: £163,000,000
DATE OF COMPLETION: OCTOBER 2010
GROSS INTERNAL AREA: 83,732 SQ. M
IMAGES: PAUL RIDDLE – VIEW
LONGLISTED FOR THE RIBA STIRLING PRIZE
LAND SECURITIES WAS SHORTLISTED FOR THE RIBA CLIENT OF THE YEAR

Given previous attempts at contemporary architecture next to
St Paul's Cathedral, this project for a shopping centre was always
going to be challenging. The radical nature of the architectural
language and approach is thus all the more remarkable. It has been
labelled a 'stealth design' by its designer, and the use of colour
fritting to pick up the surrounding stone and brick façades does
make it seem as though the new building absorbs its neighbours.

The architect has opened up the building to lost connections
across the site, and to fresh air. What's more, visitors are also
encouraged up on to the roof. Such places were once the
privilege of the lone boiler-man but are now more normally the
preserve of the rich. Instead, London has a new public space
with unique views of the river.

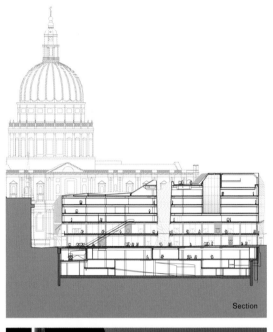

Section

RAVEN ROW
ARTILLERY LANE, E1

6A ARCHITECTS

CLIENT: RAVEN ROW
STRUCTURAL ENGINEER: PRICE & MYERS
CONTRACTOR: HARRIS CALNAN CONSTRUCTION
CONTRACT VALUE: £2,200,000
DATE OF COMPLETION: FEBRUARY 2009
GROSS INTERNAL AREA: 1330 SQ. M
IMAGES: DAVID GRANDORGE
LONGLISTED FOR THE RIBA STIRLING PRIZE

The buildings were constructed in 1690, converted into luxury shops in 1750 by Huguenot silk merchants, modernized in 1827 and, in more recent times, badly damaged by fire. Now, with supreme intelligence, subtle intervention and artful invention, they have been given new life as a gallery for contemporary art.

Wandering through the gallery spaces and up the connecting stairs, the visitor is aware of the ghosts of previous narratives. The reticent interiors, painted throughout in nearly white, are occasionally marked by bespoke raw sand-cast bronze details, such as a handrail or door knob. Two new top-lit spaces for art extend to the rear, where the new ground-floor façade to the lane is clad in iron cast in burnt timber moulds that recall the fire.

Section

RAVENSBOURNE COLLEGE
PENROSE WAY, SE10

FOREIGN OFFICE ARCHITECTS

CLIENTS: RAVENSBOURNE IN PARTNERSHIP WITH MERIDIAN DELTA
STRUCTURAL ENGINEER: ADAMS KARA TAYLOR
CONTRACTOR: BOVIS LEND LEASE
CONTRACT VALUE: £43,000,000
DATE OF COMPLETION: SEPTEMBER 2010
GROSS INTERNAL AREA: 21,500 SQ. M
IMAGES: BENEDICT LUXMOORE – ARCAID
LONGLISTED FOR THE RIBA STIRLING PRIZE

The new building is in close proximity to the O2 Arena, which sets up an unashamed clash of scale and geometry. The relatively standard programme could have produced a project that did not converse with its neighbour, let alone compete with it. FOA's design blurs the internal arrangements behind a homogeneous façade, much as the O2 does, but in a very different, very confident and curiously complementary way. It juxtaposes a plane of white fabric with a plane of tessellated panels, which somehow confuses all conventional understanding of solid, void and scale. Internally, a split-level section is divided by the atria and reconnected by bridges and floor trays. The voids connect sporadically but bottom out at different levels, informing a clear hierarchy and creating real spatial drama.

Ground-floor plan

SHADOW HOUSE
ST PAUL'S CRESCENT, NW1

LIDDICOAT & GOLDHILL

CLIENTS: DAVID LIDDICOAT AND SOPHIE GOLDHILL
STRUCTURAL ENGINEER: PETER KELSEY & ASSOCIATES
CONTRACTOR: DAVID LIDDICOAT
CONTRACT VALUE: £210,000
DATE OF COMPLETION: JANUARY 2011
GROSS INTERNAL AREA: 79 SQ. M
IMAGES: KEITH COLLIE

Living in dense urban areas requires successful compact housing models, something this thoughtful, rigorous yet inspirational house, designed and built by husband-and-wife architects, delivers admirably on a tight site and a limited budget.

With few secondary finishes, the house has a character that is entirely defined by the finished face of the black bricks, concrete and pale timber from which it is constructed. What could easily have been austere and oppressive is rich and inviting, with a sense of durability that should allow the house to mellow with age. The backdrop to the intimate living area is a picture window on to a miniature courtyard, avoiding the ubiquitous full-width openable glass wall that would be overkill in a building of this size. This house has been built on a minimum scale, but to maximum effect.

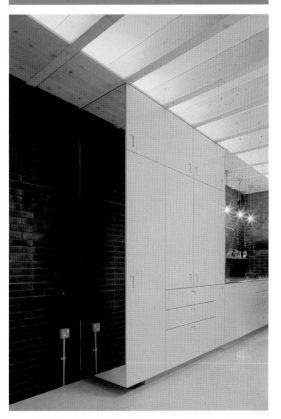

 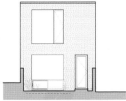

Elevations

STOKE NEWINGTON SCHOOL AND SIXTH FORM
CLISSOLD ROAD, N16

JESTICO + WHILES

CLIENT: LONDON BOROUGH OF HACKNEY
STRUCTURAL ENGINEER: MOUCHEL
CONTRACTOR: WILLMOTT DIXON
CONTRACT VALUE: CONFIDENTIAL
DATE OF COMPLETION: JUNE 2010
GROSS INTERNAL AREA: 13,450 SQ. M
IMAGES: TIM CROCKER
LONDON BOROUGH OF HACKNEY WAS SHORTLISTED FOR THE RIBA CLIENT
    OF THE YEAR

The architect has designed a series of insertions into a brutalist concrete school and made it work. The most obvious intervention is also the most engaging and thoughtful: a robust, inexpensive and low-maintenance Cor-ten steel block set on a glazed-brick plinth. This block has given the school a distinguished, powerful and lasting new identity to the street. Perhaps even more notable is the sensitivity with which other, more modest insertions have been executed. Indeed, with careful reworking of existing materials and detailing, many of these are so seamlessly integrated that it is a challenge to identify them. The work is not just a quick fix; rather, the architect has repaired, reinterpreted and preserved a building with a challenging architectural style that might otherwise have been overwhelmed or even lost.

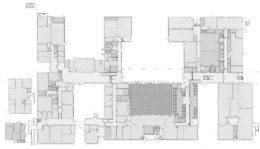

Ground-floor plan

STRANGE HOUSE
SE8

HUGH STRANGE

CLIENTS: HUGH STRANGE AND ADRIANA FERLAUTO
STRUCTURAL ENGINEER: PRICE & MYERS
CONTRACTOR: SOLMAZ CONSTRUCTION
CONTRACT VALUE: £160,000
DATE OF COMPLETION: JUNE 2011
GROSS INTERNAL AREA: 75 SQ. M
IMAGES: DAVID GRANDORGE

This enduringly likeable house has been dropped into a tight housing hinterland, surrounded by backs and boundaries. Above a highly glazed timber-framed base sits a set-back upper tier clad in profiled rigid board. This industrial-looking top gives a sense of historical continuity of use, belying the function and sophistication of the concealed base.

The cladding is one of a number of intelligent devices for constructing to budget, which also include the reuse of an existing slab as a raft foundation for the new lightweight house; a high degree and quality of off-site fabrication; and the use of Nicaraguan hurricane-felled timber. The house exudes humanity and warmth, and is the work of a confident and clever hand.

Section

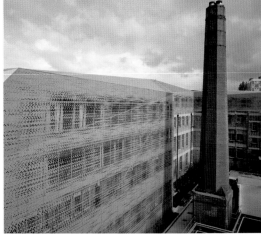

Section

TOWN HALL HOTEL AND APARTMENTS
PATRIOT SQUARE, E2

RARE ARCHITECTURE

CLIENT: MASTELLE (ZINC HOUSE)
STRUCTURAL ENGINEER: O'CONNOR SOKOLOVSKI PARTNERSHIP (OCSP)
CONTRACTOR: M.P. BROTHERS
CONTRACT VALUE: £17,000,000
DATE OF COMPLETION: APRIL 2010
GROSS INTERNAL AREA: 8900 SQ. M
IMAGES: SUE BARR – VIEW (TOP; CENTRE RIGHT; BOTTOM); ED REEVE – VIEW
    (CENTRE LEFT)

This is a project of great luxury and invention. The old Bethnal
Green Town Hall has been transformed into a mix of serviced
flats, a hotel, conference spaces, a bar and a restaurant. There
is an other-worldliness to the ensemble; different genres and
elements drift past one another in a kind of architectural reverie.
The historic marble, timber-lined and plaster interiors have been
joined by a host of bespoke elements from entire bedroom and
bathroom assemblies, as if spectral-white modernist stage sets
had somehow slipped into an Edwardian theatre. Externally, two
hugely dissimilar architectural languages have been used, that of
the existing structure and that of the new, seen in the prismatic
perforated wrapping of the new roof and the courtyard to the
rear, and they seem perfectly at ease with each other.

Elevation

AVIVA STADIUM
DUBLIN, IRELAND

POPULOUS; SCOTT TALLON WALKER

CLIENT: AVIVA STADIUM
STRUCTURAL ENGINEER: BURO HAPPOLD
SERVICES ENGINEER: ME ENGINEERS
CONTRACTOR: SISK
CONTRACT VALUE: €410,000,000
DATE OF COMPLETION: APRIL 2010
GROSS INTERNAL AREA: 66,460 SQ. M, EXCLUDING PITCH
IMAGES: DONAL MURPHY

The new 50,000-seat stadium, on the site of the old Lansdowne
Road rugby and football stadium, has been shoehorned into a
constrained, smart suburban site. Its organic form is a response
to these constraints. The stadium and its constituent components
are skilfully wrapped in a skin of translucent polycarbonate
shingles that forms both walls and roof. Unusually, the stadium
bowl is asymmetric. At the north end, where covered seating is
provided in a single tier, the roof swoops down, allowing light
into the neighbouring terraced houses and granting fans views
out of the stadium towards the city. At the south end daylight is
reflected on to the adjacent dwellings by the polycarbonate skin.

183

BODEGAS PORTIA

RIBERA DEL DUERO, SPAIN

FOSTER + PARTNERS

CLIENT: GRUPO FAUSTINO
STRUCTURAL/SERVICES ENGINEER: ARUP
CONTRACTOR: FCC CONSTRUCCIÓN
CONTRACT VALUE: €25,000,000
DATE OF COMPLETION: NOVEMBER 2010
GROSS INTERNAL AREA: 11,000 SQ. M
IMAGES: NIGEL YOUNG – FOSTER + PARTNERS
LONGLISTED FOR THE RIBA STIRLING PRIZE

A wide opening in the boundary wall connects this cathedral-like factory to the main square of the tiny town of Gumiel de Izán. First impressions of the building, which is reminiscent of a low-lying military installation, are that it is foreign to the Foster œuvre, both materially and functionally. Further observation, however, reveals that the complex process of winemaking is rationalized in a characteristically elegant and efficient manner.

The design makes use of the slope of the site to aid the winemaking process, and the colour of the Cor-ten shingle cladding and roof blends with the surrounding countryside and vineyards. The strong, sharp sunlight casts shadows on the heavy concrete walls, decorative pools of water and wall panels made of recycled-oak wine barrels, adding to the sensual richness of this emblematic building.

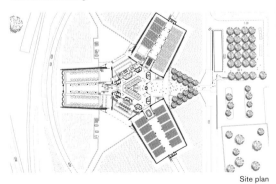

Site plan

DE PRINSENDAM

AMSTERDAM, THE NETHERLANDS

TONY FRETTON ARCHITECTS

EXECUTIVE ARCHITECT: GEURST & SCHULZE ARCHITECTEN
CLIENT: ING REAL ESTATE
CONTRACTOR: ZONNEVELD INGENIEURS
CONTRACT VALUE: €11,000,000
DATE OF COMPLETION: FEBRUARY 2010
GROSS INTERNAL AREA: 10,700 SQ. M
IMAGES: CHRISTIAN RICHTERS – VIEW

Fitting into the masterplan for a new residential neighbourhood to the north of Amsterdam, this apartment block forms a courtyard with the adjacent Álvaro Siza block that faces the river. The careful massing, the stepping of the upper levels and the rhythm of the stonework address the courtyard and wider view in a calm, honest way. The Dutch housing ideal of simple, tough, well-detailed blocks has been embraced and used to great effect. Financially, the project is, by British standards, extremely low budget. This is achieved by questioning every single component, in order to decide whether it is needed in the building. The fact that everything has to pay for itself and prove its validity is very refreshing.

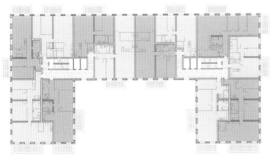

Level 2 plan

HARBOUR ISLE APARTMENTS
COPENHAGEN, DENMARK

LUNDGAARD & TRANBERG ARKITEKTER

CLIENT: SJAELSØ
STRUCTURAL ENGINEER/LANDSCAPE CONSULTANT: SCHØNHERR
CONTRACTOR: NIRAS
CONTRACT VALUE: CONFIDENTIAL
DATE OF COMPLETION: FEBRUARY 2009
GROSS INTERNAL AREA: 24,000 SQ. M
IMAGES: ADAM MØRK
LONGLISTED FOR THE RIBA STIRLING PRIZE

The masterstroke of this housing scheme of 236 social and
private flats in Copenhagen's regeneration area of Havneholmen
is the way in which the architect has challenged the masterplan,
which limited access to the water for both residents and visitors.
The detachment of a free-standing tower element from each
C-shaped block and its positioning by the water's edge created
a public footpath that diverts around the tower into and through
new, beautifully landscaped courtyards.

This scheme produces extraordinarily spacious, light-filled
flats, every one of which has two or three exterior façades and
access to at least two balconies. This is exemplary housing
architecture, and makes you realize why the Danish have one
of the highest happiness rankings in the world.

Site plan

KAUFHAUS TYROL

INNSBRUCK, AUSTRIA

**DAVID CHIPPERFIELD ARCHITECTS WITH
DIETER MATHOI ARCHITEKTEN**

CLIENT: SIGNA HOLDING
STRUCTURAL ENGINEER: WAGNER & PARTNER ZIVILTECHNIKER
SERVICES ENGINEER: A3 JENEWEIN INGENIEURBÜRO
CONTRACTOR: DIBRAL
CONTRACT VALUE: CONFIDENTIAL
DATE OF COMPLETION: MARCH 2010
GROSS INTERNAL AREA: 58,000 SQ. M
IMAGES: UTE ZSCHARNT

Using a beautifully made system of pre-cast concrete and
full-height glazing, the architecture of this department store
is strikingly and rigorously modern in a historic context. The
treatment is lifted by the use of fracture or crank lines in the
massing of the building. This subtle device does just enough to
fragment the form so it matches the scale of the rest of the street,
while retaining a unified composition. On entering, visitors find
themselves in a five-storey naturally lit and highly spatially
dynamic atrium, which follows the line of an old right of way and
provides access to all floors. The success of the scheme lies as
much in the execution as in the flexible design.

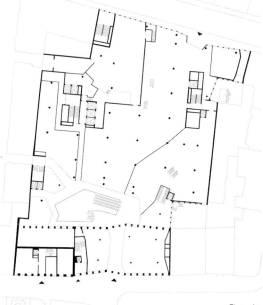

Floor plan

MIDDELFART SPAREKASSE
MIDDELFART, DENMARK

3XN

CLIENT: TREKANTENS EJENDOMSSELSKAB
STRUCTURAL ENGINEER: SCHØNHERR
CONTRACTOR: COWI
CONTRACT VALUE: £15,500,000
DATE OF COMPLETION: APRIL 2010
GROSS INTERNAL AREA: 5000 SQ. M
IMAGES: ADAM MØRK

3XN has succeeded in designing a large building that achieves a striking image for the bank, without dominating its historic context. The large sloping roof has an economical diagonal steel structure, and the eighty-three rooflights were prefabricated and all installed in three days – a remarkable achievement. The office floors step down towards the entrance and the Lillebaelt waters in a series of wide internal terraces. The journey up through the terraces is arranged as an attractive *promenade architecturale* of wide flights of steps and seats at alternate ends of the terraces. The entrance hall is large and welcoming, with very effective kaleidoscopic mirror sculptures set below glass panels in the floor. This is a memorable piece of architecture.

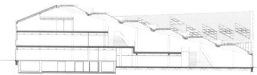

Section

SEB HEADQUARTERS

COPENHAGEN, DENMARK

LUNDGAARD & TRANBERG ARKITEKTER

CLIENT: SEB
STRUCTURAL ENGINEERS/LANDSCAPE CONSULTANTS: SLA; LUNDGAARD &
        TRANBERG ARKITEKTER
CONTRACTOR: RAMBOLL
CONTRACT VALUE: CONFIDENTIAL
GROSS INTERNAL AREA: 2711 SQ. M
IMAGES: ADAM MØRK
LONGLISTED FOR THE RIBA STIRLING PRIZE

Lundgaard & Tranberg has created two remarkable buildings
(the SEB headquarters and a smaller office building for rent),
as well as a fine new landscaped public space. This climbs via
a zigzag of paths to join the upper-level urban park that was
envisaged in the masterplan for the development of the former
freight yards. The free-form buildings, responding to sun and
views, are well composed and attractively clad with glass panels
(60 per cent transparent, 40 per cent highly insulated glass
panels of an attractive deep turquoise colour) with deeply
recessed, copper-clad joints at all floor levels. Inside the
buildings, the ground-floor plane rises in an intricate series
of steps that extends beyond the curtain wall to the stepped
landscape outside.

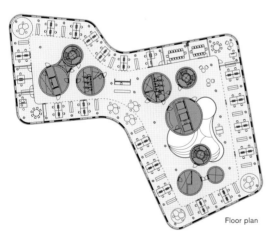

Floor plan

JAM AND KNITTING
KEVIN MCCLOUD, HON FRIBA

The word 'context' is a strange one. It is redolent of academic studies, and suggests something abstract and woolly, yet it is anything but. From St Paul's Cathedral to Heathrow Terminal 5, our buildings and our public realm have intimately reflected their setting, local geology, geography, flora and fauna; the availability of materials and of such resources as fresh water; and climate, folklore, history and culture – in other words, their context. Context is a set of many reference points, a great bundle of them.

'Context' is also an architectural term, often referring to the past and to objects that pre-exist in a place and are able to enrich it. William Morris, the designer and founder of the Society for the Protection of Ancient Buildings, wrote in the society's manifesto, issued in 1877: 'As good buildings age, the bond with their sites strengthens. A beautiful, interesting or simply ancient building still belongs where it stands, however corrupted that place may have become. Use and adaptation of buildings leave their marks and these, in time, we also see as aspects of the building's integrity.'

Something similar applies to a piece of furniture that over time suffers knocks and develops a patina of wear. But 'a chair is still a chair, even though there's no-one sitting there' (as said, not by the philosophers Descartes or Wittgenstein, but by the songwriting team of Hal David and Burt Bacharach). A chair is not rooted to a place. Its context can vary wildly. Scale architecture down to the everyday designed object, and the arguments of context become progressively weaker. But let us try scaling them up. Everything Morris said about buildings also applies to the street, the square and the city. He might equally have said: 'As good streets and cities age, the bond with their sites strengthens. Use and adaptation of cities leave their marks and these, in time, we also see as aspects of the city's integrity.'

Let us accept that a historic building has a positive contribution to make to our world, that a beautiful old pub, an eighteenth-century town hall or a wonky corn exchange cheer us up when we see them. It might be a step too far to agree with Morris that a true understanding of history is the key to happiness, but the layering and the complexity of our built environment provide depth, interest and relief, like a moist and flavoursome layer cake of reference. We are creatures who demand complexity: our eyes are accustomed to texture and grain.

Not that history alone should assume the burden of providing all that layering and interest. To think it should is a mistake made by many conservationists who assume that by reproducing history you can reproduce its meaning. You might be lucky enough to evoke an echo or memory, a pleasing association. You might make a pleasant enough brand-new 'Georgian' street, but it would be about as layered, moist and flavoursome as a cream cracker. And bizarrely, the products of this sort of thinking are based on an extraordinarily narrow period of history that seems to finish arbitrarily around 1830.

We should be looking around us for other clues when we design places, buildings and houses. More than twenty-five years ago, in a response to the homogenized international modernist style of building that dominated the twentieth century, the critic Kenneth Frampton wrote an essay about what he called 'critical regionalism', in which he suggested that architecture should respond to the particular character of a place; he did not call it vernacular. Only now are we arriving at a point where we have the confidence to develop Frampton's ideas: Deborah Saunt, the architect and teacher, describes what is happening as 'architecture that engages with local context and represents a situated response'. What matters is the collective memory and perceptions of cities and society, because, despite what Margaret Thatcher told *Woman's Own* magazine in 1987, there is no such thing as society.

The word that best describes this role that buildings and places can play is 'narrative'. The power of narrative, of storytelling in buildings and in the built environment is unlimited; as with all storytelling, it is this power that sparks the imagination. This helps us to make sense of history, and history helps us to make sense of the present. 'Narrative' is another word for 'context', because it implies that the context of a place need not always be tangible and visual, but might be mythical. Of course, history can be rewritten: there are plenty of deracinated buildings that are merely historical façades propped up by modern office blocks behind. There are plenty just left to moulder with their roots intact; some are gently repaired, others over-restored. Some stop history in its tracks, some reproduce history, others leave it to accelerate, and yet others fake it. And who is to say which is true? Context can be created in a narrative as well as found in a place. Humankind has a fantastic ability to plan, organize and make places out of nothing, out of no context at all, and by doing so to create a new narrative – in other words, a sense of place. The move from chaos to order, from noise to narrative, is the clear expression of human creativity. So how do people react to places rich in contextual tension?

Recently I went to stay in Mumbai's Dharavi, one of the largest slums in Asia and a place full of myth and dirt, to try to begin to understand this for myself. A television crew came with me to help record my impressions and the profound effect the slum had on me. Dharavi is a reputed hellhole with a population that nobody can precisely quantify. Some 300,000 people are on its electoral register, but many people say that residents number two or three times that figure. Aid workers put the number at up to a million people in Dharavi's square mile. As a comparison, the average population density of Mumbai as a whole is 76,000 per square mile; New York has 26,000 people per square mile, London 13,000.

Dharavi is a place of contradictions, a place where you go to understand what paradox is. It is officially a slum for several technical reasons: it has rudimentary sanitation and poor health facilities, and its residents have few, if any, formal property rights. This may partly explain why residents will not invest in their homes but will pay special attention to the beauty and cleanliness of their bodies and clothes instead.

I spent two weeks in the company of Dharavi's residents, and discovered some of the things that make the place tick and also some of its contradictions. The first contradiction is that Dharavi looks like a hellhole but is an economic miracle, with an estimated annual turnover of $500 million out of one square mile of shanties. Number two is that it may be riddled with illiteracy and health-care issues (plague, cholera and tuberculosis abound, as they did in the London slums that Dickens described in his novels), but its citizens seem to be reasonably happy and crime is extremely low. Number three is that despite attempts by the Mumbai government to knock down and redevelop Dharavi (it lies at a convenient nexus of infrastructure just north of the city centre, and therefore sits on what is now some of the most valuable land in India), the slum has attracted the attention of planners and architects from around the world who would prefer to work with and improve what is there. And number four is that nobody, it seems, from outside Dharavi ever goes there, not even from downtown Mumbai. Mumbaians see Dharavi as a threat, a slum, a dangerous place and a source of vice and crime; and yet a large number of its residents work in the distant office blocks and city businesses, leaving their huts and shanties in their suits early in the morning.

Commentators, planners and sociologists see a 'protocity', a civic entity in formation. Town planners like the chaotic, plan-free and dynamic way in which Dharavi's residents organize their lives and neighbourhoods. It is as if those planners were being magnetically, and perversely, drawn to the polar opposite of their own discipline. Prince Charles, champion of sustainable model communities, is also a fan of Dharavi, describing it as an adaptable place in 'balance' and 'harmony', with 'built-in resistance' and 'durable ways of living', and built on 'an intuitive grammar of design' and a 'resilience of vernacular standards'.

Development is planned for Dharavi, of course. Developers don't do 'messy'; they prefer things to be tidy. Development has to fit within a red line on the plan and be highly marketable, not scrappy round the edges. The trouble is that human beings happen to be scrappy round the edges by nature. It is what gives rise to interesting places, idiosyncratic homes and streets with higgledy-piggledy charm.

As urbanists Rahul Srivastava and Matias Echanove, who have been working in Dharavi for a decade, organizing participation exercises with local people, put it: 'The first mistake of virtually all slum redevelopment schemes, no matter how well intentioned, is to start from scratch instead of using existing structures and patterns as a starting point. ...

'The end result of most redevelopment projects is a series of grids in every direction, up, down and sideways, that erases all the existing formations imprinted on the territory. The constant movement of people within urban spaces and across neighbourhoods, as well as fresh migrations – factors that every city has to reckon with – find no legitimate expression. Nor does the versatile use of space, a trademark of slum life.'

What is needed is a third way, a road less travelled, a reinforcement and support of what is already there. But that would be difficult, expensive and politically less appetizing to do. Treading the sensitive, architectural middle ground between doing nothing and radical overhaul would require a lot of effort, but it is already being done. The old fishing village of Koliwada in Dharavi is now protected, and non-governmental organizations have been working with communities there for several years, empowering them to control their own destiny. The result is that the neighbourhood feels just that little bit more spruced up, as though residents understand and cherish what it is they have.

This approach, one of respecting the existing, of conserving what is good and polishing it up alongside the new and then stitching the two together, is not anti-development. It is open-minded, it refutes dogma; it involves communities and requires that design be far more inclusive; and it is a lot harder to get right. It should produce gentler architecture that is more responsive to where it is, and can produce buildings and places that do not shout.

An illustration of this thinking is the scheme that my development company, Hab, built in Swindon in partnership with the GreenSquare group of housing associations. The surprisingly modest scheme was designed by Glenn Howells Architects, and the landscape and public realm are by Studio Engelback. It is based partly on Swindon's traditional railway cottages that are so admired by locals, but we are evolving, not slavishly reproducing, that language, with designs that are ecological, spacious, light and adjusted to the patterns of contemporary life. And rather in the way architect Ralph Erskine and his team did at Byker in Newcastle in the 1970s, it avoids displacing individuals, families and communities.

Our scheme in Swindon is a response to the strong market-driven culture that has grown in the last twenty years in the housing sector. These nakedly commercial values have now seeded their spores across all sectors; that culture is so strong that neither the recession, nor the Design Council and CABE, the RIBA or even government low-carbon legislation can among them kill it off. Its leitmotifs are speed, ease of delivery and sales. It does not like the fuzzy, delicate weaving of the kind of housing I appreciate. It does not like jam, because that is sticky and messy, and does not have the time to take up knitting, which is home-made and laborious and is done in the evening.

Houses should not be pastiches of local vernacular building types, but their design ought to pay respect and homage to where they are, the history of the place, its landscape and culture. But we need buildings that are designed to be of their time. Human beings carry the curse of memory and nostalgia. We need very little: warmth, shelter and food just like other animals, plus the psychological needs of comfort and support. It is our job as house-builders, together with the architects and landscape architects we employ, to take responsibility for all these human needs. This means extracting as much sense and narrative out of a place as possible in order to make a scheme feel special and rooted to where it is. If Hab is going to be involved in transforming green fields into a housing estate, the first thing we would have to do is to enshrine every tree and hedge and then fit the houses in between. We would have to use the field gates as the cues for our roads, and the streams as the lines of our water courses. Because that is how we keep a sense of the history of a place and the history of its use, which all adds up to a more intelligent narrative or understanding of what it has been. The result can be likened to a palimpsest – a document on parchment that has been scraped clean of the ink of a previous use but has retained a shadow of what had been there. If context provides the framework, then the glue is the rich social relations that architecture hopes for.

On this basis, how happy do people feel when they live in a place that is not the product of 'architecture' or even a formal design process? The answer, it seems, is quite happy. The buildings of Dharavi may not be proper architecture, but they do cater for people's needs. And it is salutary to remember that over the other side of the sub-continent, in the self-contained kingdom of Bhutan, the king's policy puts gross national happiness above gross domestic product. Now there's a blunt pencil for an economist to sit on.

Mumbai is no pleasure dome. It is the forcing ground for Indian capitalism, and the relentless pursuit of money – whether in order to survive, hoard or reinvest – characterizes the place. The great difficulty Dharavi faces is how to protect and nourish the social glue and strong sense of family and community that make it a happier place in which to live, while at the same time tempering the material ambitions and acquisitive instincts of its residents and the wider city at large.

What we in the West need to do is the same, but in reverse. We need to curb our enthusiasm for status, the acquisition of stuff and materialism, while developing a keener, richer, more elaborate set of connections with the people who live around us and with the place we inhabit. We need more knitting and more glue. And we need architecture and design to help us achieve these things, because that is what architecture and design are for.

This essay is based on the text of Kevin McCloud's 2010 RIBA Annual Lecture.

THE ROYAL GOLD MEDAL

ELIZABETH WALDER, MA, FRSA

The Royal Gold Medal was established by the RIBA in 1848, and is still awarded and celebrated today. It was conceived as a result of a conversation between the then President of the RIBA, Earl de Grey, and Prince Albert.

The idea for a Gold Medal had come about in 1846, twelve years after the foundation of the RIBA. Originally, it was to be awarded to the winner of a competition to encourage young architects to design 'a building suitable and practical to house the Institute and its daily operations' – an idea that received royal approval from Buckingham Palace. Eleven designs were submitted, but – according to the RIBA's centenary history – 'they missed the mark so entirely: they were, most of them, so grandiose and expensive – in short, they so widely disregarded the conditions imposed, that the medal was not awarded. This fiasco sealed the fate of the junior members of the profession in regard to the medal and it was decided to award it in future not to the immature work of the young but in recognition of the actual achievements of the older men [sic].' (In fact, to date, shockingly, no woman has won the medal in her own right.)

Earl de Grey's fresh approach was communicated to Queen Victoria via Prince Albert. It was agreed that the medal should be 'conferred on some distinguished architect for work of high merit, or on some distinguished person whose work has promoted either directly or indirectly the advancement of architecture'. This has remained the basis of the criteria to this day.

The RIBA commissioned William Wyon, Chief Engraver of the Royal Mint, to execute the medal. The Vice-President of the RIBA, Ambrose Poynter, designed the reverse, showing a laurel wreath encircling text and the RIBA's coat of arms. The name of the winner is inscribed around the edge of the medal. Today the Royal Gold Medal is still made by the Royal Mint. As the gift of the monarch, it shares a coveted status with twenty-four other Royal Prize Medals awarded annually by Her Majesty The Queen. As originally conceived, previous winners include architects, engineers, historians, writers and theorists (see pp. 247–49).

Nominations for Royal Gold Medallists are made by members of the RIBA in the third quarter of the year prior to the year of the award. Names are considered by a distinguished panel chaired by the President of the RIBA and including architects and non-architects from the United Kingdom and overseas. One name is presented to Her Majesty for approval, and the winner is announced in October. The formal presentation is held the following February.

This year's Honours Committee, which chooses the Medallist and the International and Honorary Fellows (see pp. 204–209 and 210–16), comprised the following:

RUTH REED
RIBA PRESIDENT, 2009–11

EDWARD CULLINAN, CBE
ARCHITECT
EDWARD CULLINAN ARCHITECTS

MAX FORDHAM
ENVIRONMENTAL ENGINEER
MAX FORDHAM

EVA JIRICNA
ARCHITECT
EVA JIRICNA ARCHITECTS

LAURA LEE
CLIENT
MAGGIE'S CENTRES

CHRIS WILKINSON, CBE
ARCHITECT
WILKINSON EYRE ARCHITECTS

SIR DAVID CHIPPERFIELD, CBE: THE ROYAL GOLD MEDAL CITATION
DEBORAH SAUNT

David Chipperfield occupies a unique position, managing to represent architecture beyond the boundaries of a region, a nation or even the specifics of the European continent. He is a British architect for the twenty-first century, working globally and with a number of offices overseas, but always grounded in the United Kingdom. His work is internationally celebrated and yet remains timeless, beyond fashion, and it is both contemporary and fresh while embodying the persistent power of classicism, but without the insistence on a strict or didactic language.

The places Chipperfield creates are sensitively formed to respond to context and are essentially urban, always being read as part of a bigger landscape. This is not iconic attention-seeking architecture that focuses on itself; instead the work, be it a single new building or the sensitive restoration and re-imagining of an old building, always mediates between the individual user and the city. The materiality his practice has developed over the past three decades pushes beyond 'white modernism' to a manifest palette of subtle textures, materials and sensations: from plaster, stone, concrete and timber through to glass, meshes and perforated flat metals, and often in dialogue with the existing fabric of a neighbouring or host building.

Experientially, Chipperfield's buildings are both light and solidly permanent, combining contradictory qualities where delight and seriousness inhabit spaces simultaneously. At every level his work exhibits perseverance and commitment, qualities all too often lacking in contemporary design. It is also an architecture with a determination to resolve detail and strategy at the same time, yet it avoids reverting to cliché. Chipperfield's RIBA Stirling Prize-shortlisted Museum Folkwang in Essen epitomizes this.

Chipperfield's superb architectural *œuvre* has been hard won. Being a groundbreaking architect is not easy. Chipperfield has built his reputation on international competitions, rising to the occasion time and time again to resolve complex briefs and sites with a precise conceptual clarity. This clarity then informs the resulting architecture so that it is at once humanistic, abstract and monumental. Chipperfield's work is an art form, as his exhibition at the Design Museum in London in 2009 showed so clearly, and it leaves the viewer asking questions, wanting more.

Gormley Studio, London, 2001–03

Neues Museum, Berlin, Germany, 1997–2009

Shortlisted competition entry for Tate Modern, London, 1994

BBC Scotland, Glasgow, 2001–06

Chipperfield has been a mentor to young architects around the world and inspires great work in others. His relevance goes further than the making of architecture: he informs its culture. So why is he a mentor? How does he manage to be so significant in an age of icons, fashions, allegiances and brands? And how does he avoid the pitfalls of both superstardom and the smaller world view of parochial practice?

Chipperfield has achieved his position by bringing architecture to the fore. His work is at all times about pushing for the best-quality architecture possible, irrespective of the particular challenges of a project. He champions architecture plain and simple, and is a testament to the persistent and dogged determination and inspirational talent required to make great work. He simply did not give up, sell out or change tack. He crafted his career. The work matured, got stronger and continued to be commissioned. It has seemed at times that Chipperfield's work was destined not to materialize in Britain, apart from such smaller projects as his beautiful shop interiors, his studio for Antony Gormley and the River and Rowing Museum in Henley-on-Thames in the 1990s; but finally the time has come. This year, 2011, saw the opening of the Chipperfield-designed Hepworth Wakefield in Yorkshire and Turner Contemporary in Margate, Kent: local, specific projects to counterpoint his *grandes œuvres* in Berlin, Anchorage and Iowa. The list goes on, and future projects of great stature can be glimpsed emerging round the world.

Beyond this string of elegant and uncompromisingly modern projects that are now garnering accolades, Chipperfield's influence is linked with the dissemination of ideas; his projects have appeared in books and journals from the earliest shows in 1985 at the 9H Gallery, London (of which he was co-founder), in libraries and in exhibitions. With his major show at the Design Museum he took the display of his architecture to another level, combining giant models, working drawings and small maquettes. And his role is not simply about showing his work. He has always demonstrated generosity in his persistent commitment to teaching around the world, in tandem with running a hugely successful and demanding practice. This is no mean feat. Chipperfield's contribution extends to architectural discourse through lectures, and sitting on architectural juries for major competitions. He has been assessor in competitions for the New Art Gallery in Walsall, West Midlands, and, in Lausanne, Switzerland, for the Rolex Learning Centre and a new art gallery project. He has chaired the jury for the European Union's Mies van der Rohe Awards. His curating of the Royal Academy Summer Exhibition in 2010, under the title of *Raw*, again showed his commitment to extending architecture to a new audience without compromise.

Chipperfield has often been asked why more great architecture does not seem to happen in Britain, when we boast some of the world's best architects. But instead of being critical he simply gets on with it, proving that, against the odds, good architecture does have a place here. We need people like David Chipperfield, to remind us that the struggle can be worthwhile.

SIR DAVID CHIPPERFIELD
IN CONVERSATION WITH TONY CHAPMAN

TC: In your early career you worked with both Richard Rogers and Norman Foster, and they were obviously concerned with expressing new technologies. What do you think you learned from them? And how did you react against them?

DC: I don't think I reacted against them, I just took them for what they were. When I worked for Richard, he had just finished the Pompidou Centre in Paris, and I thought this was an unbelievably exciting project – I still do. I was pulled in to work on the competition for the Lloyd's Building, and it was a tiny office. I learned from Richard this unique thinking, and it was an eye-opener to see, within a constrained professional circumstance, that these dreamers were also very practical. And then at Foster's it was a similar experience, in a way.

TC: The two offices must have had very different atmospheres.

DC: Yes, probably as a reflection of the two individuals who ran the ships. Richard's is a more 'hairy' operation, more personal, and Norman's was very slick.

TC: There's a bit of both in your work still, a bit of hairiness and a bit of the organization, isn't there?

DC: I think I probably took something from both of them. And both offices set the bar high.

TC: When you went out on your own in 1984, it was the middle of a recession, pretty much as we are today. It must have been hard?

DC: Well, it lowered all our expectations; we never thought we'd get a job. I think mine was the generation that woke up to a different relationship with patronage and foresaw years of house conversions and shop interiors – not just as a stepping stone, but as a profession.

TC: Of course it was partly the economy, and partly the way architects were perceived.

DC: Yes, if one were a conspiracy theorist one would think that all these things were aligned, including Prince Charles. But in a way I'm not sure one could really blame the public for the general attitude towards the profession at that point.

TC: Architects brought it on themselves, you mean?

DC: I think a lot, yes. I think that essentially what Prince Charles said wasn't really wrong at that time, modern architecture was rubbish. When I started working, at the beginning of the 1980s, anything modern was seen very negatively, even modern furniture. So we had a lot of ground to make up.

TC: But you and a few others consciously set out to rethink the modernist position, didn't you, with the 9H Gallery in London and the magazine?

DC: Yes, although history always looks easier in hindsight, and

I'm not sure I can claim that I set out to do anything. I was fortunate to meet the students working on 9H, such people as Ricky Burdett, Wilfried Wang, Joseph Paul de Santos. I was running a little practice and was conscious of not giving in to the excesses of postmodernism. It was interesting, through 9H we looked at Europe and suddenly we saw people like Álvaro Siza doing good modern architecture, but it was much richer and more thoughtful and intense, and contained many of the things for which modern architecture had been blamed for not having.

TC: So architecture was beginning to take its place in the cultural scene?

DC: Yes, all of a sudden people were quite interested in talking about architecture and trying to help you. So in some sense, I think the Architecture Foundation was an interesting child of 9H; in a way it got its credibility from 9H.

TC: And you wanted to get people talking about architecture?

DC: Well, we don't all build Pompidou Centres or Bilbaos [Guggenheim Museum] or MAXXIs [Rome]. We're not all building the singular cultural object, of which everyone can say, 'The Trojan horse has arrived', and 'Wow!' What happens when you're building in Henley-on-Thames; what happens if you're building in Des Moines, Iowa; what happens when you're building not a national building but a local library? You can't skip that dialogue with the public. They are part of the dialogue, even though they are not properly part of the planning process. So, therefore, I feel that the architect is the one who has to carry that voice, the voice of the cynical passer-by, the voice of the person who doesn't actually live in that building but walks past it every day, because they too are your clients.

TC: But doesn't that second-guessing lead to a kind of conservatism?

DC: Absolutely. I think as animals we're conservative; even in our radicalism we're conservative. But although I might take a conservative position, it's not conservative in terms of history; it's conservative only in terms of accepting certain rules and judgements, which I believe carry meaning with them. I don't believe that things are without meaning.

TC: Everything has a history, hasn't it?

DC: Absolutely!

TC: And the history is made up of the lessons that you've learned.

DC: And those lessons are part of the continuity, they're part of meaning, and they're part of what we expect, and they allow us to understand things. I think that within that discussion, you can shock people, you can do things they're not expecting. But what touches you when, for example, you read a novel? It's because you've found something in the human condition that we can all share. Modernism is all about trying to prove things were different, and I think that we should be just as interested in what things are similar and continuous.

TC: But modernism is also a part of history.

DC: Now modernism is, yes, absolutely. You now get people who are super-conservative preserving modernist monuments. If you lobby to save Robin Hood Gardens [a 1960s council housing estate in Poplar, east London], are you lobbying for modernism? Or are you lobbying for conservatism?

TC: Possibly a more useful thing to talk about than conservatism in architecture is modesty. Both you and your architecture are often described as modest – too modest?

DC: No. I have a family that ensures my feet, if not the rest of me, stay firmly on the ground. I think we, architects, have to explain ourselves. I think there is a role for the flamboyant; we need flamboyant architects and flamboyant architecture. But I think we also need architecture that doesn't necessarily occupy that position all the time. We mortals have to do other things that bind things together. I think we've got plenty of architects who can do those one-off things. I'm interested in another type of architecture.

I wouldn't say that I want our work to be characterized by the word 'modest', but I would actually like it to be characterized by the idea of being humane. For me, within the humane tradition of architecture there was always a narrative about the position of the individual, and the idea of bringing things back to the individual, and the modern movement safeguarded that as well. There is architecture as a spectacle to be looked at from a distance, the 'cathedral dimension', one could say the 'wow factor' – a horrible expression, I cringe when anyone says it. I suppose it's this idea that architecture is something away from you, like a mountain. What I'm more interested in is architecture that puts you in a position. We're sitting here in front of a little window, the window is made of two leaves, those leaves are both the size that a person could lift. I can stand at that window, that's my window to the world. This room and this window put me in a relationship.

TC: So architecture is a frame?

DC: Architecture is a mediator between us fragile, sensitive human beings who don't quite know what we should be doing, and this big, wide, frightening world.

TC: A few years ago, when Álvaro Siza received the Royal Gold Medal, I explored with him the idea of 'slow architecture' – similar to 'slow cooking'. Is that something that resonates with you?

DC: Of course, but we're just not allowed it anymore. I remember being shown around Siza's unfinished School of Architecture in Porto by Joseph Paul de Santos, when the concrete structure was in place. I asked why there was no one on the site, and he said, 'Well, they are waiting for Siza to finish the drawings of the façade.' So he hadn't detailed a façade yet. I love the idea that the client was waiting for the architect to catch up with the construction. I think if anybody combines the double aspect of architecture, of being both humane and novel, and in a way just slightly out of one's reach, it's Siza. He always puts the individual

in a very interesting position, slightly alienated but not very. I think history will show he's been probably the greatest architect of the twentieth century.

TC: Let's turn to Germany; it's a kind of spiritual home for you, isn't it?

DC: I've really enjoyed working in Germany, and I think it's influenced our work enormously. There's no doubt about it, the office would be a very different place if we hadn't done the Neues Museum in Berlin.

TC: And that masterplan for the Museum Island is contextualism writ large, isn't it?

DC: Yes, but I was always interested in context. I think that in Germany context is very heightened and articulated; it's not just physical, it's also intellectual. So the demand on architecture there is very different from anywhere else, and I think one has to confront the issue of language more than one would in most other places. Because meaning is paramount, and Germans want to know fundamentally what something means, what an action means.

TC: Can you talk about the Marbach Museum of Modern Literature, in that type of context?

DC: It's a tiny building, and the positive reaction was surprising, because the museum reintroduces a sort of classicism, and post-war Germany was very uncomfortable with classicism, for very good reasons. What's interesting is that it probably took a foreigner to bring back to Germany an architectural language that harks back to a classical tradition. I think as architects we like to talk about architecture, and if anybody were to ask, 'Why does your building look like that?', they'd get all sorts of reasons. It could be about structure, it could be about circulation, it could be about materiality, it could be about distinguishing itself.

TC: It's a British trait, to be scared of ideas, or of talking about ideas.

DC: Yes, but I think everybody is, I think all architects are. 'Why does it look that way?' makes us squirm in our seats. I think that in Germany you do have to answer that question. Also, if you're on Berlin's Museum Island, it's even more important; you've got to deal with language. I suppose we do talk about things here, but in a way it became a polemicized thing: either something is historical or it's new. We never really looked at the idea that modern architecture could be in some sort of continuity.

I think we're always struggling with these disparate realities. Architectural history has always seen architecture as having some aspiration to permanence, and we still hold on to that idea. We don't consider buildings in the same way as cars. Whatever building you see, whatever expression it has, it's still lumpen, it's still made out of mass. Whether a building has a glass skin or a solid skin, underneath it's still the same building. It's set in concrete, it's not going anywhere. And therefore I'm completely fascinated intellectually by the idea that architecture is not permanent any more, it's on legs and it can be picked up …

TC: Portable architecture …

DC: Experimental architecture. What Foster, Rogers and Archigram were doing, buildings sitting on stilts: you can imagine

City of Justice, Barcelona, Spain, 2002–09

Anchorage Museum at Rasmuson Center, Anchorage, Alaska, United States, 2003–09

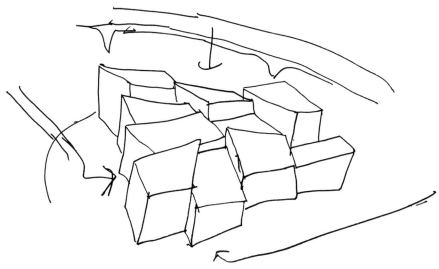

Sketch for the Hepworth Wakefield, West Yorkshire, 2011

those buildings being picked up and moved, but we don't do it. So the idea that architecture aspires to permanence, luxuriates in substance and has the ability to erode and mature over time, pushes us away from the other tendency we have to confront, which is the idea of architecture as assembly and of the dematerialization of architecture. Where do we sit between these two contradictory positions, one stating that architecture inevitably has mass and permanence, and the other that it is a language resulting from the process of putting things together?

In all our projects, our office tries to deal with that struggle between openness and lightness on the one hand, and substance and permanence on the other. There are certain buildings that have clearly gone to the substance side; the Hepworth Wakefield is undeniably a substantial block carved out of concrete. There are others, such as Museum Folkwang, that are clad in cast glass, which has both lightness and quite an interesting solidity. For me, that is where architectural tension lies.

The industry is pushing us a certain way, and the larger-scale the project is the more we're pushed. If you're doing a little house in Islington, in a way you can almost build it by hand. But if you're contracting a larger project, the concerns of industry come into play quite quickly and you have to address them. And I think it's an intellectual issue as well, it goes back to your question about whether I'm conservative or not. Yes, I am, because I think that there is continuity, but at the same time I do think we should be taking advantage of advances in technology. The question is, how do we take advantage of things we are being offered, how are we in control compositionally and conceptually?

TC: What does winning the Gold Medal mean to you?
DC: Well, I get my name put up with the likes of Álvaro Siza. It's

not something I ever expected, and I probably don't deserve it, but it's nice to be identified with having done work of quality, which I presume the award must be for. All prizes are questionable in some sense, in that you're not quite sure what the jury was thinking about that day, but I'm grateful to receive it on behalf of the office. I don't think that we've necessarily done extraordinary work, but, within this quite difficult Anglo-Saxon climate of commercialism, as architects we have endeavoured to maintain a body of work. I am quite proud of the fact that our office, over at least twenty years or so, has produced a body of work that I think is serious. I don't know whether it's important, but it's serious, and we've probably flown the flag a little bit for architecture in England, which is a difficult place in which to practise. And I don't know whether it's getting much easier.

River and Rowing Museum, Henley-on-Thames, 1989–97

Liangzhu Museum, Hangzhou, China, 2003–07

THE RIBA INTERNATIONAL FELLOWSHIPS

Throughout its history, the RIBA has honoured men and women who have made a major contribution to the world of design and, in particular, architecture. Any architect outside the United Kingdom who is not a UK citizen, has a demonstrable interest in the objectives of the RIBA, and exhibits distinction and breadth of contribution to architecture may be elected an International Fellow of the RIBA. The lifetime honour, conferred annually, allows recipients to use the initials Int FRIBA after their name. Prior to 2006, such people were elected Honorary Fellows; in 2006, with the creation of the new honour, all architect Honorary Fellows, including non-UK surviving Royal Gold Medallists, were made RIBA International Fellows.

Of the eight architects made International Fellows in 2011, five work in partnership. They come from six different countries, and their work not only represents the spirit of their countries, but also transcends it to become truly international in its reference and influence.

This year's RIBA International Fellows were chosen by the Honours Committee, which also selects the Royal Gold Medallist and the RIBA Honorary Fellows (see pp. 196–203 and 210–16). For the list of committee members, see p. 196.

ABDEL WAHED EL-WAKIL
EGYPT

Abdel Wahed El-Wakil's work is an extension of the ideas of Hassan Fathy, the father of modern Egyptian architecture. In El-Wakil's work the Arabian ideas of brick domes and arches are extended to large buildings. The attraction of such forms is that they generate structures with the robust separation of inside from outside that is necessary for sustainable buildings in extreme climates.

A graduate of Ain Shams University in Cairo, El-Wakil set up his own practice in 1971. He has built fifteen mosques in Saudi Arabia and others in Bahrain, Brunei and Johannesburg, as well as private houses and commercial buildings across the world. When he won the first Aga Khan Award in 1980 for his Halawa House in Agamy, El-Wakil generously shared the award with his mason Ala-el-Din Moustafa. He won a second Aga Khan Award in 1989 for the Corniche Mosque in Jeddah.

El-Wakil was one of the first architects to understand sustainability, particularly in hot climates. His latest building is in England: the Oxford Centre for Islamic Studies, a £75 million student residence with teaching facilities, which uses load-bearing brick with no steel or concrete in the structure. It blends the architecture of the Oxford college with that of Islam's classical period: the quadrangle with the Islamic garden, the bell tower with the mosque. It stands as a symbol of reconciliation between two religions and two ancient traditions of scholarship. The commission owes something to the fact that the centre's patron is HRH The Prince of Wales, who is an avowed admirer of the architect's work, and who wrote in his book *A Vision of Britain* (1989) that a house by El-Wakil on the Greek island of Hydra epitomized the qualities of traditional architecture.

Corniche Mosque, Jeddah, Saudi Arabia, 1988

ÉDOUARD FRANÇOIS
FRANCE

Édouard François was born in Paris in 1957. He is one of the chief international protagonists of green architecture, and his work focuses on matter, context, use, economy and ecology, following the preoccupations of sustainable development.

As a technologist and an artist who studied town planning, François is interested equally in the science and the art of architecture. He revels in complexity. 'Man can live solely within architecture', he says. 'He needs a complex building which must be decorated. Only in this way can he be happy.'

François became widely known for his Château le Lez housing in Montpellier (2000), 'the building that grows'. Its exterior walls feature rocks held in place by a stainless-steel net covered in plants. There followed his Tower Flower overlooking a park in Paris (2004), an apartment block that is completely veiled in white bamboo and typifies his decorative approach to architecture. The walls were poured randomly – one batch of concrete being grey, the next white – giving a hazy appearance to the building. The balustrades are decked with huge flowerpots made of lightweight concrete and planted with bamboo.

In 2006 François tackled the problem of how to humanize car parking with a 1600-place underground car park in the Place des Ternes in Paris's 17th arrondissement, clad with jungle-like plants. His work responds in a chameleon-like way to its surroundings, so that when he was asked to design an ecological eighty-room hotel on the Champs Elysées in Paris, he responded to the lack of a natural context, producing a grey concrete replica like the ghost of the monumental façade of the old Fouquet Hotel near by.

François's latest project is Eden Bio (2008), a Parisian housing block of 100 social apartments and ateliers for artists, with community rooms and a restaurant. The buildings are faced with a timber scaffold colonized by thousands of wisteria plants.

Tower Flower, Paris, France, 2004

MA YANSONG – MAD ARCHITECTS
CHINA

Ma Yansong is a Chinese architect whose work expresses the tension between the individual imagination and the needs of society as a whole. He was born in Beijing in 1975 and studied at Yale University School of Architecture. He graduated with a Master's degree in 2002, did an internship with Peter Eisenman in New York and then worked with Zaha Hadid in London. He moved back to Beijing in 2004 and set up MAD, a design office dedicated to innovation in architectural practice. MAD's design philosophy integrates futuristic architecture with a contemporary interpretation of the Eastern spirit of nature. All MAD's projects aspire to protect and maintain a sense of community and orientation towards nature, offering a new architecture that sees buildings not as isolated objects but as part of the natural environment.

The firm's works include the Hutong Bubble 32 in Beijing; a museum in Erdos (Dongsheng); Sinosteel's headquarters in Tianjin; three cultural buildings in Harbin; and Fake Hills, a residential complex in Beihai. Ma's Absolute Towers (2006), in an expanding suburb of Toronto, was the first project in the West to be commissioned from a Chinese architect. Consisting of two twisting towers that reach fifty and fifty-six storeys respectively, it is a residential landmark that strives for more than simple efficiency. Journalists subsequently dubbed the scheme the 'Marilyn Monroe towers' because of its slinky forms.

Since 2006 MAD has produced a number of exhibitions: *Mad in China* and *Mobile China Town*, both at the Venice Architecture Biennale, and *Mad under Construction* at the Beijing Tokyo Art Projects Gallery. MAD's *Floating City* was showcased at the Danish Architecture Centre in Copenhagen in 2007–08. Most recently, Ma Yansong collaborated with Olafur Eliasson on the large-scale installation *Feelings are Facts* at the Ullens Center for Contemporary Art in Beijing. The practice's first monograph, *Mad Dinner*, was published in 2007.

Absolute Towers, Toronto, Canada, 2006

WINY MAAS, JACOB VAN RIJS AND
NATHALIE DE VRIES – MVRDV
THE NETHERLANDS

MVRDV stands for Maas, Van Rijs and De Vries, the three Dutch architects who founded the Rotterdam-based firm, which is known as one of the Super-Dutch practices, in 1991. Their work explores the tension between the interests of the client and those of the user, and the laws that govern the process. The resulting buildings – such as the early Wozoco housing in Amsterdam (1994–97) – are at once challenging, anarchic, pragmatic and humane. In the Dutch tradition of theoretical projects intended to provoke politicians and stimulate debate is the book *Metacity/Datatown* (1999), which proposed a series of what-if? scenarios.

Other early projects include offices for the Dutch broadcaster VPRO in Hilversum (1993–97) and the Dutch Pavilion at the Hanover World Exposition 2000 (1997–2000). MVRDV recently completed its first project in the United Kingdom, working with Living Architecture, an organization initiated by the writer Alain de Botton, which has persuaded a series of great architects to design houses for holiday rental,

thus introducing people to the joys of modern architecture (see p. 138, The Balancing Barn).

MVRDV's current projects include a masterplan for Greater Paris; a public library in Spijkenisse, western Netherlands; Rotterdam Market Hall, a public market and apartment building; and a House of Culture and Movement in Frederiksberg, Denmark.

In February 2011 Winy Maas was invited to address the European Parliament, taking the rare opportunity to tell MEPs that 'It is now almost forbidden to be visionary. In Europe we always have to build small. Big is now only on the other side of the planet.' He also criticized what he called the 'rush for sustainability': 'When green is put on top of old buildings as a mere add-on it produces insanely ugly buildings and much confusion. Instead of this, the demand for green should rather lead to new architecture.'

Wozoco, Amsterdam, The Netherlands, 1994–97

KJETIL T. THORSEN AND CRAIG DYKERS – SNØHETTA NORWAY

In 1987 Kjetil Thorsen and Øyvind Mo set up a collaborative studio with a group of landscape architects, with the aim of incorporating architecture and landscape architecture into one design process. The firm took the name Snøhetta arkitektur landskap, after one of Norway's highest mountains.

Two years later Thorsen in Oslo and Craig Dykers in Los Angeles formed a team to enter the competition to design the Library of Alexandria in Egypt; it won, beating off 1400 other entries. The Alexandria team then joined Snøhetta, which now had eight equal partners with diverse backgrounds, fostering a collaborative notion that remains a key feature of the practice. Snøhetta's Scandinavian heritage provides it with a special understanding of social and environmental issues, which form the intellectual basis of all its work.

The Library of Alexandria houses eight million books and has a main reading room beneath a 32-metre-high glass-panelled roof, tilted towards the sea like a sundial 160 metres in diameter;

the walls are of grey Aswan granite, carved with characters from 120 different human scripts. The project also includes a conference centre; specialized libraries; four museums; four galleries for temporary exhibitions and fifteen for permanent exhibitions; a planetarium; and a laboratory for the conservation of manuscripts. A remarkable achievement for a first project, it took fourteen years from competition to completion.

Snøhetta's next major scheme was completed in a mere ten years: the Oslo Opera House, with a main auditorium of 1350 seats and smaller theatre with 400 seats. The project was finished ahead of schedule, and under budget. The opera house won the culture award at the World Architecture Festival in Barcelona in October 2008 and the Mies van der Rohe Award, the European Union Prize for Contemporary Architecture, in 2009. It is the largest cultural building to be built in Norway in 600 years.

Oslo Opera House, Norway, 2008

THE RIBA HONORARY FELLOWSHIPS

In 2011 the RIBA awarded twelve new Honorary Fellowships to men and women from a wide range of backgrounds, including project managers, writers, film-makers, clients, landscape architects and designers, engineers, environmentalists, politicians and architectural historians.

RIBA Honorary Fellowships reward the particular contributions made to architecture in its broadest sense: its promotion, administration and outreach; its role in building more sustainable communities; and finally its role in the education of future generations. The lifetime honour, conferred annually, allows recipients to use the initials Hon FRIBA after their name.

All these people, be they practitioners or commentators, have done much for architecture. In their very different ways, they have all helped to improve the quality of design and influence the delivery of the built environment in a sustainable and creative way.

This year's RIBA Honorary Fellows were chosen by the Honours Committee, which also selects the Royal Gold Medallist and the RIBA International Fellows (see pp. 196–203 and 204–209). For the list of committee members, see p. 196.

CLIVE BIRCH
PROJECT MANAGER

Clive Birch has been championing architecture and architects for more than thirty years, during a distinguished career as project manager and as one of the founding partners of Buro Four. He has taken this advocacy to places architects find hard to reach: highly commercial private developments (working on some of them with Stuart Lipton, Hon FRIBA); Vodafone's World Headquarters with Fletcher Priest Architects; early Private Finance Initiative (PFI) projects, such as Crawley Schools with Feilden Clegg Bradley Studios; and many others. As a result, he was invited to become one of the first ten Commission for Architecture and the Built Environment (CABE) enablers, and proved to be a very effective champion of design quality.

Buro Four, one of the most respected project-management firms, has a particularly good reputation among architects. Birch undertook the PFI schools programme for West Sussex Council, working with both contractors and design practices. He is involved in the Department for Children, Schools and Families' (now the Department for Education) Academies programme and, with Buro Four, has helped to build over twenty academies across England.

Because of his extensive experience with schools procurement and his early work as part of the Building Schools for the Future (BSF) programme, the RIBA asked Birch to help to tailor the institute's Smart PFI proposals to BSF. He did this with great patience, strategic nous and diligence. He devised a convincing workplan for the RIBA's procurement proposals and then argued the case with Partnerships for Schools, the non-departmental public body set up by the Labour government to deliver the BSF programme. As a result, we have come a long way in the campaign for a better and faster process with closer engagement of architects, design teams and clients in the key early stages (although, inevitably, there is much more to do). And all this was achieved by Birch working pro bono.

LUCY BULLIVANT
ARCHITECTURE CURATOR, WRITER AND CRITIC

Lucy Bullivant has worked as a London-based architecture curator, writer, critic, guest lecturer and adviser since 1987. She has forged connections with leading museums, galleries, cultural institutions, publishers and corporate bodies around the world, advancing projects that highlight the qualities and skills of the United Kingdom's architects.

In all her projects, be they writing, facilitating, curating, advising, lecturing or architectural judging (for the Architectural Association, the RIBA and the Berlage Institute), Bullivant has consistently advocated higher design standards and experimental multidisciplinary strategies. Her work as a critic and writer, as well as a regular chair of events and guest lecturer internationally, brings fresh research ideas to bear on every task, and means that she is well suited to the role of advancing the public's understanding of the place of architecture in society.

Bullivant's international exhibitions and conferences (as well as their related publications) have covered groundbreaking and yet popular projects – as evidenced by the large number of people who attend. They have featured leading and emerging international practitioners from a range of disciplines, and have

dealt with topical subjects relating to architecture's role as a social art, including its 'new pragmatism'; its relationship with landscape architecture; alternative strategies in the design of public housing; the role of responsive environments; and the cultural history of children's environments in and beyond the Western world.

Bullivant has always striven to bring important topics and individuals to public attention, not relying on commissions, but also working speculatively on self-generated projects. She is widely respected for her work to build awareness of the cultural value of architecture and for her investigations into emerging modes of practice and their social effects. Her consistent publication in leading specialist magazines shows her global commitment to communicating topical concepts, views and projects to an international audience.

The RIBA is pleased to recognize Bullivant's independent, yet deeply collaborative, cross-cultural international work.

TONY CHAPMAN
FILM-MAKER, WRITER AND RIBA HEAD OF AWARDS

The excellence, integrity and high reputation of the RIBA's awards system owes a great deal to the energy, skill and determination of Tony Chapman. On his watch, 'Stirling' has grown from a bright idea to one of the great showcases for architecture, captivating the general public as well as the cognoscenti.

Since joining the RIBA in 1996 from the BBC, where he produced a number of films on architecture (including – with then RIBA President Maxwell Hutchinson – *The Max Factor* (1989), a modernist riposte to Prince Charles), Chapman has continued to make excellent use of his broadcasting skills. Not only is his footage seen at RIBA presentations and dinners, but it also forms part of the judging process for many awards, and is often used by Channel 4 and the BBC. As the maker of focused low-budget films on architects including James Stirling, Herzog and de Meuron, Edward Cullinan, Álvaro Siza, I.M. Pei and David Chipperfield, he has helped to record the advances in modern architecture. A filmed interview he did with Oscar Niemeyer featured in the New York Architecture and Design Film Festival

in 2010. His love of architecture and passion for communicating it show particularly in such filmed interviews, enabling him to gain remarkable insights into the working practices and design philosophies of his subjects.

Chapman is also the author of a string of architecture books, building on the awards programme. The hallmarks of his writing are a clarity of argument and language and an ability to get to the nub of an issue. This all-too-rare combination marks Chapman out as an exceptional writer and champion of the world of architecture and the people involved in it.

The RIBA is pleased to recognize Tony Chapman with an Honorary Fellowship for his special contribution to the communication of architecture to the public.

MICHAEL GAZZARD
FOUNDER OF THE BRITISH HOMES AWARDS

Michael Gazzard's background is in the motor industry, and he developed a passion for good architecture in later life. He was the force behind the foundation of the Manser Medal, and of the British Homes Awards, which were until 2010 sponsored by the *Mail on Sunday* and are now supported by the *Daily Telegraph*. Prior to that, Gazzard and his company Custom Publishing ran the National Homebuilder Design Awards – the first attempt to kick-start an interest in design among house-builders. This is not an arena in which architecture is much discussed (nor indeed is the important topic of house-building often the subject of architects' conversations – it works both ways), but Gazzard's awards generate a very high level of interest among readers. With the support of the man who has chaired the programmes for most of their existence, past RIBA President Michael Manser, Gazzard's awards have encouraged and sometimes shamed developers into taking design seriously and employing architects.

In the last few years sustainability has been promoted as the theme in both these sets of awards, producing some excellent responses. The winning entry in the Home for the Future design competition in 2007, the Gaunt Francis-designed Green House,

has been built at the BRE Innovation Park near Watford and is being tested – but not yet to destruction.

Gazzard has brought two things from his marketing background in the car industry: an understanding of the importance of public relations and marketing in persuading people to buy architecture, and an appreciation of the lessons one design business can teach another. He has, for example, always been keen to reward the use of new technology and modular systems. His success is in taking his passion for architecture and design into everyday house-building.

MOIRA GEMMILL
CLIENT, THE VICTORIA AND ALBERT MUSEUM

As the Victoria and Albert Museum's Director of Projects, Design and Estate, Moira Gemmill is one of the key people behind the £120 million FuturePlan, intended to bring the V&A into the twenty-first century. The first phase (2000–09), which touched on 70 per cent of the museum (including many galleries, the shop, the cafe and the education centre), culminated in the opening in December 2009 of the Medieval and Renaissance Galleries, designed by the architectural practice MUMA, little known at the time of its appointment. The second phase (2010–19) began with the new Ceramics Galleries, which were designed by OPERA Amsterdam and opened in June 2010. The other key project in Phase 2 is the restoration of the V&A Cast Courts.

Gemmill was born in Kintyre and read for a degree in art and design at Glasgow School of Art, specializing in graphic design and photography. She joined Aberdeen Art Gallery and Museums as an Exhibitions Officer, staying for a decade, which culminated in the opening of a new Maritime Museum in the city. She moved south in 1998 to take up the post of Head of Exhibitions and Design at the Museum of London.

In 2002 Gemmill went to the V&A as Head of Design. Using her graphics training she was able to take a new and considered look at how the museum presented itself to the world. It has taken her seven years to change the way visitors feel on entering the museum and what they take away from the newly interpreted collections. Gemmill drove the Medieval and Renaissance Galleries' design team, whose three partners are also Scottish and trained at Glasgow School of Art, to find coherence in a disjointed collection of spaces and artefacts. Together they have created a suite of ten thematic galleries from existing spaces as well as reclaimed storerooms and offices.

ANDREW GRANT
LANDSCAPE ARCHITECT, GRANT ASSOCIATES

Andrew Grant studied landscape architecture at Heriot-Watt University and Edinburgh College of Art between 1977 and 1982. He spent three years working in Doha on projects for His Highness the Emir of Qatar, before joining landscape architects Nicholas Pearson in Bath from 1985 to 1997. He formed Grant Associates in 1997 to explore the emerging frontiers of landscape architecture within sustainable development. The consultancy specializes in the creative design of both urban and rural environments, and is involved in projects throughout the United Kingdom, Europe and the Far East, working with some of the world's leading architects and designers.

Grant Associates has built up a reputation for innovative, ecological design and the ability to shape useful and sustainable landscapes with distinctive contemporary character. The practice is concerned with the connection between people and nature, and has been consistently involved in cutting-edge design projects stemming from a concern for the social and environmental quality of life, searching for bold and imaginative solutions to complex and demanding briefs.

The firm has experience in strategic landscape planning, masterplanning, urban design and regeneration, and landscapes for housing, education, sport, recreation, visitor attractions and commerce. It has worked for clients as diverse as the National Trust, Urban Splash, Rolls-Royce, English Partnerships, the Foreign and Commonwealth Office, Wessex Water and the National Parks Board of Singapore, where the practice has an office.

Grant's approach is driven by a fascination with creative ecology and the promotion of high-quality, innovative projects. He has built up experience in all scales and types of project, from sub-regional planning to the detailing of the smallest piece of new landscaping. He is a member of the Commission for Architecture and the Built Environment's specialist unit Space, and of the South West Regional Design Review Panel.

Grant was a key part of the team (which included Feilden Clegg Bradley Studios, Maccreanor Lavington and Alison Brooks Architects) that was awarded the RIBA Stirling Prize in 2008 for Accordia, a new housing project in Cambridge.

JAMES LOVELOCK
SCIENTIST AND ENVIRONMENTALIST

James Lovelock's first interest is the life sciences, originally in the form of medical research but more recently in that of geophysiology, the systems science of the earth. His second interest, that of instrument design and development, has often benefited the first. His influence on architecture is indirect but powerful, in that his thinking has forced architects to consider the impact of their designs on the planet.

Lovelock is best known for developing the Gaia Theory, which asserts that Earth's physical and biological processes are inextricably bound to form a self-regulating system. It also states that living organisms and their inorganic surroundings have evolved together as a single living system that has an impact on the conditions of Earth's surface. The term 'Gaia' refers to the Greek earth goddess and was suggested by Lovelock's friend the novelist William Golding. Lovelock has written three books on the subject.

Lovelock graduated in chemistry from Manchester University in 1941, then took a PhD in medicine in 1948 and a DSc in biophysics in 1959. Since 1964 he has conducted an independent practice in science, although continuing his teaching in the United Kingdom and the United States. He is the author of more than 200 scientific papers, covering medicine, biology, lunar and planetary research, instrument and atmospheric science and geophysiology. He has applied for more than forty patents, mostly for detectors for use in chemical analysis, one of which, the electron capture detector (ECD), confirmed the common survival of pesticide residues and polychlorinated biphenyls (PCBs) in the natural world and was important in the development of our environmental awareness.

Lovelock was awarded Fellowship of the Royal Society in 1974, the Volvo Prize for the Environment in 1996 and the Blue Planet Prize in 1997. He was made a CBE in 1990, and in 2003 a Companion of Honour.

GWYN MILES
CLIENT, DIRECTOR OF SOMERSET HOUSE TRUST

Gwyn Miles has been a catalyst for regeneration and change at a series of important British cultural institutions. She has been Director of the Somerset House Trust since 2006, promoting architectural exhibitions and finding interested creative tenants, such as the Sorrell Foundation, the Courtauld Institute and London Fashion Week, and is in the process of commissioning important new projects, all with the aim of unlocking ever more of the cultural riches of Somerset House for the benefit of the public. It now receives over one million visitors a year.

Miles began her career by training as a scientist, and she has worked in museums since 1972, first at the Ashmolean Museum in Oxford, then at the Royal College of Art, where she was responsible for the new centre for research and the conservation of art. She moved in 1985 to the Victoria and Albert Museum as Deputy Keeper of Conservation, and in 1989 was made Surveyor of Collections and Project Leader for the development of the museum's new centre for research and conservation. She developed a programme of travelling exhibitions for the V&A collection, including a William Morris retrospective and a major exhibition about the V&A, *A Grand Design*.

In 1995 Miles took over as Head of Major Projects at the V&A. She was the project director for the major re-display of the British Galleries project, which opened to great critical and public acclaim in 2001. She was then instrumental in developing the ambitious new masterplan for the museum and subsequent commissions within the building, of which Phase 1 was completed in December 2009 with the opening of MUMA's Medieval and Renaissance Galleries.

The gestation period for the kinds of project Gwyn Miles has instigated throughout her career is complex and very long, but she has the perspicacity and organizational skills to ensure a lasting legacy.

DAN PEARSON
LANDSCAPE DESIGNER

Dan Pearson is a landscape designer much loved by architects. He has worked with Conran & Partners, Feilden Clegg Bradley Studios and Hopkins Architects, among others. His work enhances their buildings, rather than fighting them; it seats them within their environment, offering views and framing the buildings instead of hiding them. His landscaping of the RIBA Stirling Prize-winning Maggie's Centre in Hammersmith by Rogers Stirk Harbour + Partners and the gardens for John and Frances Sorrell's Stirling-shortlisted house are among the best examples of this design skill.

Introduced to gardening as a child, Pearson later completed a Royal Horticultural Society apprenticeship at Wisley in Surrey. He still cites his early experience and practical grounding at Wisley as having given him a breadth of knowledge that sets him apart from other landscape designers.

Pearson designed his first garden at the age of seventeen. He worked at the Royal Botanic Garden in Edinburgh for a year, then completed a three-year degree course at Kew Gardens. During this time he created a garden for Frances Mossman at Home Farm in Northamptonshire. It was there that he perfected the naturalistic planting style for which he is known.

Pearson has produced five award-winning show gardens at the RHS Chelsea Flower Show, and runs an established landscape design business. He is an engaging and informative presenter of programmes on BBC2, Channel 4 and Channel 5 television. He writes a weekly gardening column for *The Observer* and has written for the *Daily Telegraph* and the *Sunday Times*. He wrote *The Essential Garden Book* (1998) with Sir Terence Conran and is the author of *The Garden: A Year at Home Farm* (2001) and *Spirit: Garden Inspiration* (2009), which explores his passion for the *genius loci*. Pearson is a tree ambassador for the Tree Council and was a judge in the 2011 RIBA Stirling Prize.

CHRIS TWINN
ENVIRONMENTAL SERVICES ENGINEER, ARUP

Chris Twinn is Director of the Sustainable Buildings Team at Arup. In 2004 he was appointed to the Design Review Committee of the Commission for Architecture and the Built Environment (CABE), bringing sustainability and environmental awareness to the closer attention of the panel. By taking into account the importance of the building envelope, master-planning and wider context, Twinn aimed to bring these topics to the fore as vital influences in the early stages of design.

Twinn's background is in architectural engineering, and after gaining professional qualifications in building services he turned his attention to multidisciplinary design, building physics and sustainability. He has spent some thirty years concentrating on the design and construction of environmentally aware projects, and he has a special interest in the planning system, with its ability to shape sustainable communities.

Twinn continues to be directly involved in design work, from individual homes to large-scale urban masterplanning, and has been responsible for the first new homes to achieve Level 6 of the Code for Sustainable Homes (an initiative of the Department for Communities and Local Government), as well as for numerous eco-towns and cities in the United Kingdom and across the world. Among the many projects in which he has been involved are: Kingspan Lighthouse and the Barratt Green House (both at the BRE's Innovation Park near Watford); Hanham Hall Carbon Challenge; Dongtan Eco-City; BedZED; Gallions Park; Ashford ZED; Thames Gateway Zero Carbon Development; Portcullis House; King's Cross Central; and Stratford City.

As well as being a member of CABE's Design Review Committee, Twinn sits on the RIBA Sustainable Futures Committee, the BRE Global Sustainability Board and numerous other professional committees. He contributed an incisive essay to *Architecture 09*, with the aim of 'keeping the awards on their toes in matters of sustainability'. He is a regular adviser to central and local government in the United Kingdom, and is in increasing demand as such around the world.

ED VAIZEY MP
MINISTER FOR CULTURE, COMMUNICATIONS
AND THE CREATIVE INDUSTRIES

Ed Vaizey was elected as the Member of Parliament for Wantage and Didcot in 2005. Until the general election in 2010 he was the Conservatives' Shadow Minister for Culture, looking after arts and broadcasting policy. Then, for a matter of days, he had responsibility in the coalition government for one of his first loves, architecture, a subject he had come to know and to ask searching and intelligent questions about during his shadow ministry. However, a possible perceived conflict of interest in the portfolio of his colleague Jeremy Hunt meant that ministerial responsibilities were reshuffled, sadly for Vaizey and sadly for architecture, not least at a time when the profession needs all the friends it can get.

Vaizey is now Minister for Culture, Communications and the Creative Industries, a job that is split across two departments: Culture and Business. His portfolio includes the arts, the media, museums and galleries, telecoms and broadband, the digital switchover, the creative industries and libraries. In the current economic climate it will take all his well-honed political, diplomatic and communications skills to fight to maintain adequate investment for the many subjects he covers.

Born in 1968, Vaizey studied modern history at Merton College, Oxford. He subsequently spent two years working for the Conservative Party's Research Department, before training and practising as a barrister. In 1996 he gave up law for the more flamboyant world of public relations, becoming the director of a highly successful agency in London. After eight years he moved back into politics and, with a parliamentary seat in mind, became chief speech writer for Michael Howard, then Leader of the Opposition. During his time in public relations and backstage politics, Vaizey developed a career as a freelance political commentator, writing regularly for *The Guardian*, and appearing on such television programmes as *Despatch Box* and *The Wright Stuff*. Even though the built environment is no longer within his brief, Vaizey still sees architecture as a formative influence in all our lives.

DR SUSAN WEBER
ARCHITECTURAL HISTORIAN

Susan Weber was nominated for an Honorary Fellowship for her work as an architectural historian and in particular for promoting the study of British architectural history in the United States.

Weber is the director and founder of the Bard Graduate Center (BGC), New York, and Iris Horowitz Professor in the History of the Decorative Arts. Over the last few years she has worked tirelessly to bring knowledge of British and European architects, patrons of architecture and mostly British architectural history not only to the American public but also to a broad international audience through a programme of exhibitions, publications and lectures at the BGC. Subjects include *Le Corbusier Before Le Corbusier: Applied Arts, Architecture, Painting, and Photography, 1907–1922* (2002); *William Beckford, 1760–1844: An Eye for the Magnificent* (2001), which was also shown at the Dulwich Picture Gallery in London; *The Anglo-American Century 1814–1914: Designing an Era* (1999); *Josef Frank, Architect and Designer: An Alternative Vision of the Modern Home* (1996); and three major exhibitions also shown at the Victoria and Albert Museum, *A.W.N. Pugin, Master of Gothic Revival* (1995), *James 'Athenian' Stuart*

1713–1788: The Rediscovery of Antiquity (2006) and *Thomas Hope: Regency Designer* (2008). The RIBA was a major lender to all these exhibitions. The next projected joint exhibition (2013) with the V&A, and to which the RIBA and its staff are contributing loans and catalogue essays, will be on the great eighteenth-century designer William Kent. The accompanying publications, which Weber edits and often co-authors, are monuments of scholarship.

Other British architects whom it is proposed should be the subject of exhibitions at the BGC are all figures that are heavily represented in the RIBA's collections. They include Alfred Waterhouse, William Burges, Philip Webb and Charles Voysey. Susan Weber's contributions to scholarship have been recognized by the American Society of Architectural Historians and the Victorian Society in America.

THE RIBA PRESIDENT'S MEDALS STUDENT AWARDS

Since the 1850s the RIBA has been awarding the President's Silver Medal to reward student work. In 1986 the institute first awarded both the Silver Medal, for Part 2 design work submitted by a student, and the Bronze Medal, for Part 1 work. In 2001 a Dissertation Medal was awarded for the first time. The aims of these prestigious awards have always been to promote excellence in the study of architecture, to reward talent and to encourage architectural debate worldwide. Past RIBA President's Medallists include David Adjaye, Sean Griffiths, Simon Hudspith, Mouzhan Majidi and Ole Scheeren.

Each year, students from schools of architecture in the United Kingdom and abroad hope to be selected by their school to enter their work for the medals, and for the opportunity for their work to be recognized and publicly exhibited. In 2010 a record 270 schools of architecture from more than sixty countries were invited to nominate their best student work.

In 2010 the judging panels selected eleven projects to receive awards. Medals were awarded in three categories: the Bronze Medal, for best design project at Part 1; the Silver Medal, for best design project at Part 2; and the Dissertation Medal. In addition, there were commendations and sponsors' awards.

Jack Hudspith from the Mackintosh School of Architecture (Glasgow School of Art) won the Bronze Medal for his project 'Cook School', and Jonathan Schofield from the University of Westminster won the Silver Medal for his project 'Creative Evolution: Silvertown Ship-breaking Yard'. Clare Richards from the University of Westminster won the Dissertation Medal for her work 'Happy Communities'.

The winners received their medals and commendations in front of an audience of more than 400 people at a prestigious ceremony held at the RIBA on 1 December. Previous guest speakers at the event have included Norman Foster, Alex James, Mark Lawson, Richard MacCormac, Richard Rogers, Martha Schwartz and Paul Smith.

Chaired by Oliver Richards (ORMS and RIBA Vice-President for Education), the judging panel for the design projects comprised Marcus Fairs (founder and editor-in-chief of Dezeen.com) and Francine Houben (Mecanoo Architecten, Delft, The Netherlands). The jury for the Dissertation Medal, chaired by Professor Peter Blundell Jones (University of Sheffield), comprised Professor Adrian Forty (The Bartlett, University College London), Matt Gaskin (Oxford Brookes University) and Ruth Slavid (freelance architectural writer, editor and consultant).

Atkins is the principal sponsor of the President's Medals. In 2010 the awards were also sponsored by the Institute of Materials, Minerals and Mining (IOM3), Callprint and the SOM Foundation; *RIBA Journal* was the media partner.

The President's Medals website (presidentsmedals.com) features all the nominations since 1998.

Cook School, Perthshire

COOK SCHOOL
PERTHSHIRE

STUDENT STATEMENT BY JACK HUDSPITH
MACKINTOSH SCHOOL OF ARCHITECTURE
(GLASGOW SCHOOL OF ART)

The Cook School is a place where fifteen people work –
growing, preparing and cooking food – live and learn 'off-grid' for
a year. It is in Braco in rural Perthshire, a distinctive landscape
that is home to one of the finest examples of a Roman fort in
Britain. When I went there I was struck by the beauty of the fort,
and I wanted to respect its authority as a ruin. It was for this
reason that I felt it essential not to overpower the site's ancient
authority but to enhance its special qualities.

The Cook School building is based on simple architectural
principles that respond to their context through light, material and
function. It sits gently within its delicate setting, but continues and
amplifies its surroundings. I drew on the passive ideals of hermits
and monastic communities as ancient environmental precedents.
The scheme reinterprets and becomes part of the lost ramparts,
which were destroyed by previous settlements, through the use
of materials and forms that work well close to the ground. The
building hence creates a direct relationship with the growing and
cultivation of food at a very human scale.

I also drew on the work of a number of architects I admire.
I looked at how Enric Miralles used the landscape surrounding
his Scottish Parliament in Edinburgh, and how he connected the
building to its site. I also looked at the ways in which Louis Kahn
and Peter Zumthor allowed light into the vaults and other
important areas of their buildings.

The Cook School is a simple project: it is about light,
materials and place, and it is about how people connect with
their surroundings. I wanted to make a place to which people
would be interested in going.

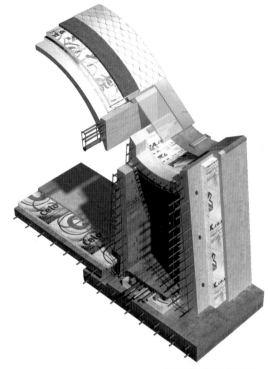

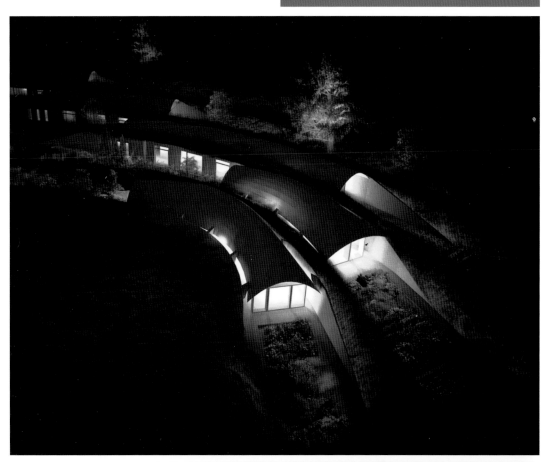

SILVER MEDAL

CREATIVE EVOLUTION
SILVERTOWN SHIP-BREAKING YARD

**STUDENT STATEMENT BY JONATHAN SCHOFIELD
UNIVERSITY OF WESTMINSTER**

'What we do depends on who we are; but it is necessary to add
also that we are, to a certain extent, what we do, and that we are
creating ourselves continually.'
Henri Bergson, *Creative Evolution* (1907)

After the closure of the Royal Docks, Silvertown in east London
went from being part of the largest dock in the world to being
a ghost town, a place of memory. Not only will Silvertown ship-
breaking yard provide the local community with opportunities
for highly skilled jobs, but also, through the creative process
of playing with, testing, experimenting with and reconstructing
ship elements, there will emerge new individual and communal
identities for Silvertown's inhabitants. The project may be
categorized in three stages.

Ships are broken up through a complex process that takes
place inside the breaking chamber. In a reversal of the traditional
construction process, this specially designed channel extracts
lighter elements first and the heavier structural parts last.
Elements are either recycled by being sold to a scrapyard and
flea market, or used for experimental reconstruction.

Local inhabitants experiment with transforming elements
of broken ships into new potential forms of architecture. This
process takes place inside the Ludic Chamber of the 'Trawler
Jig', where elements are suspended.

Construction rules are defined through a library of hybrid
details that outline the system, the rules of 'the game', but do
not completely define the output of this creative process. The
resultant architecture is then placed around the site by the Trawler
Jig. As the community becomes more developed and experienced,
the architecture produced is improved and updated.

Through this highly skilled creative and evolutionary
process, a new identity is created for Silvertown. With the local
inhabitants' creative potential achieved, their lives are enriched.

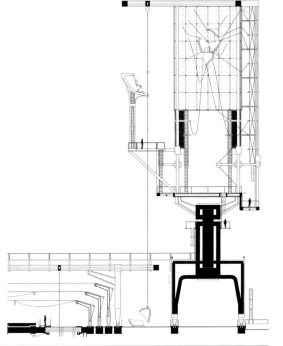

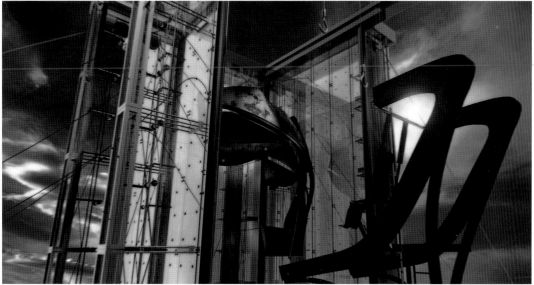

HAPPY COMMUNITIES

**STUDENT STATEMENT BY CLARE RICHARDS
UNIVERSITY OF WESTMINSTER**

Architects, politicians and planners believe that well-designed built environments have a transformative effect on people's lives. They see themselves as integral to the process of creating socially sustainable communities – an objective that is backed by legislation and passed down in the delivery requirements for housing projects.

Yet, while billions of pounds are spent on house building and regeneration, in the belief that successful communities can be created by design, it does not seem to make communities better. Curious that both thriving and failing communities come in many guises, I decided to investigate the relationship between their built form and their social circumstances.

Observational accounts, written over 150 years, identified some of the features of successful communities and the underlying causes of their failure. Historical precedents revealed the extent to which planned environments have contributed to the success of communities. I focused on two communities in London's East End: the Holly Street Estate in Hackney, and Bromley-by-Bow in Tower Hamlets. Holly Street has undergone a costly and well-designed redevelopment; Bromley-by-Bow has received minimal funding for piecemeal improvement. Yet Holly Street's social problems persist, while Bromley-by-Bow is experiencing a revival, through locally generated social enterprise.

This investigation reveals a gulf between well-intentioned aspirations and the reality of community life. We have a poor understanding of what constitutes a 'happy community', and an inflated sense of the built environment's ability to create it on its own. The characteristics that decide whether communities will thrive or fail are not solely dependent on their physical form; there are social factors, over which designers have little control, that must be addressed first.

Communities evolve slowly, from a strong social base. Architects can contribute to their success, but only in conjunction with others: by taking account of local, social and historical context; and by engaging collaboratively with people to create the physical conditions in which they can function and thrive.

Bromley-by-Bow, Tower Hamlets

Holly Street Estate, Hackney

THE HOUSING DESIGN AWARDS

DAVID BIRKBECK, HON FRIBA

Another high level of entries for the Housing Design Awards demonstrates what the panel of judges has been seeing for a number of years: that the design and the delivery of new housing in England continue to increase in quality, a conclusion that is also borne out by high levels of resident satisfaction.

This year there are again project awards for schemes that have received planning permission but are not yet built. In addition, the judges visited seventeen completed schemes in a three-day marathon. Some schemes show how to deliver a complete package of sustainable-development measures within standard cost parameters, while there are also great examples of 'urban mending' on both large and small scales.

Back-to-backs, 1960s futuristic glass pavilions, council houses, brickwork in 1970s-style earthy hues, bachelor pads, maisonettes, deck-access apartments, tenement blocks: all of these appear among entries for the 2011 awards, rescuing concepts once consigned to the dustbin. Remember when Margaret Thatcher asked Alice Coleman to review what had gone wrong with council housing, and the resulting book, *Utopia on Trial* (1985), buried deck access? This year it is ubiquitous, notably at Peabody Avenue (p. 233) and even more surprisingly in almshouse-type designs for the ageing population.

Housing design responds quickly to financial and political anxiety by walking away from anything flawed, without looking to mend the flaw. The Housing Design Awards often help to overcome that knee-jerk response by rewarding those who have gone back and fixed the problem. The perception that a point block should never again house social tenants lasted from the late 1960s to 1995, when Lifschutz Davidson won a Housing Design Award for Broadwall on London's South Bank. The scheme bookended terraced houses with a modest tower, with views on to the Thames, and it still looks as good as ever. The same practice has this year stacked 'unpopular' maisonettes in four-storey blocks to look like Georgian terraced town houses. So, is Cambridge & Wells Court (p. 239) set to have similar influence?

Reinvention quickly rehabilitates. This year's entries are remarkable for signalling a return to brickwork, chosen in the first instance for its reputation for low maintenance needs. But it is clear that many practices are also using it as part of a new aesthetic that treats crisp modern masonry as an authentic local style for our shires and cities. Such reinventions are destined to have a profound influence on our new-build stock.

Just as innovation is common in housing design and delivery, the Housing Design Awards have made their own innovations. Now entirely self-funded, the awards remain the government's long-standing flagship housing awards programme. The Housing Design Awards are now online in their entirety (hdawards.org). Available on the website is a series of films by architectural photographer Tim Crocker featuring residents as well the architect/developer teams. All the entries are now also made available in an electronic database on CD to help the widest possible audience to see what the judges have seen. And an app allows those interested to view each of the winning and shortlisted schemes in minute detail, with the facility to zoom into the photographs, plans and layouts.

GRANARY WHARF
LEEDS

CAREYJONES CHAPMANTOLCHER; CZWG
ARCHITECTS; ALLIES AND MORRISON ARCHITECTS

CLIENT: ISIS WATERSIDE REGENERATION
CONTRACTORS: ARDMORE CONSTRUCTION; LAING O'ROURKE
PLANNING AUTHORITY: LEEDS CITY COUNCIL
IMAGES: DENNIS GILBERT – VIEW (P. 230); HUFTON + CROW – VIEW (P. 227;
   BOTTOM; OPPOSITE; P. 231)

Granary Wharf is the name of a 0.8-hectare site masterplanned by CareyJones ChapmanTolcher between Leeds railway station, the Leeds–Liverpool Canal and Holbeck village. The site has 282 new apartments housed in a twenty-one-storey circular tower called Candle House designed by CareyJones and a fourteen-storey stepped block called Waterman's Place by CZWG.

Concepts for both buildings were inspired by Leeds city architect John Thorp, and particularly informed by his well-known petal-diagram sketch of how the city's quarters have a core characteristic. CareyJones's new tower is close by Holbeck's ornate Victorian chimney stacks known locally as 'Giotto' and 'San Gimignano', and was expected to be called 'Pisa', something the architect played on by staggering the vertical alignment to create the impression of leaning. There is yet more

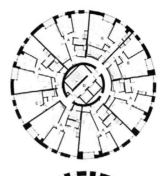

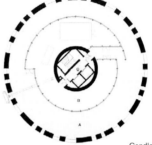

Candle House floor plans

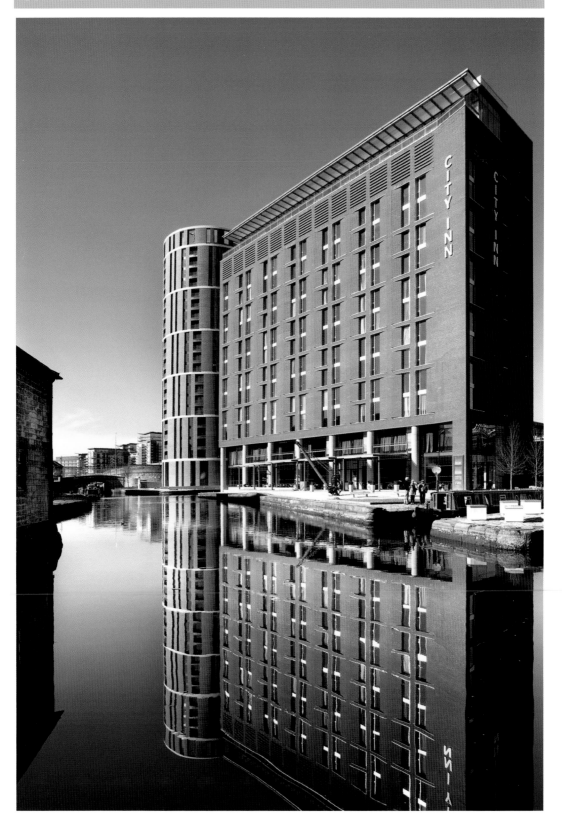

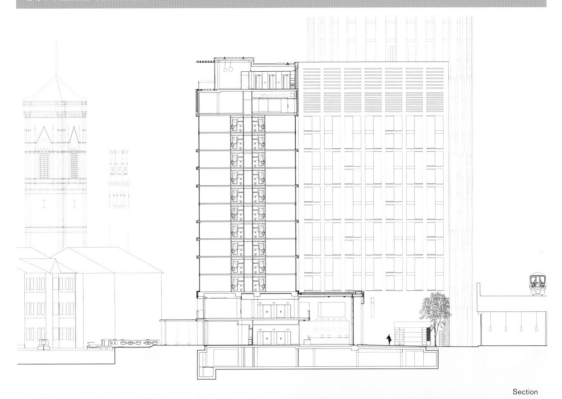

Section

fun at Waterman's Place, which is faced with timber on the stepped south-facing façade so that as it weathers to flinty grey it increasingly resembles the crags of the Dales, which can be seen from its upper floors.

Apartments in circular buildings often suffer from pizza-slice floor plans. However, CareyJones has glazed large parts of the broader outside wall to invert the issues of daylighting found in single-aspect units. There are a small number of 28-square-metre studios in the tower without balconies, although these are flattered by the same ratio of fenestration. Otherwise all apartments are large, and include the city's only three-bed units, at up to 139 square metres. Apartments have copper balconies, recessed ones on the tower and projecting ones on Waterman's Place, where the units also enjoy huge terraces over the steps to the south-facing elevation.

Between the two apartment blocks stands a new hotel designed by Allies and Morrison, and some converted railway arches. All of the twelve leased commercial premises open on to high-quality public realm created by Capita Symonds that picks up on the area's industrial heritage, using steel, granite and stone. The judges were especially impressed that all three buildings have generous shared outdoor spaces at upper levels; Candle House has a roof terrace for all residents. All apartments have the level of specification usually found in small, more exclusive developments.

ARUNDEL SQUARE
LONDON N7

POLLARD THOMAS EDWARDS ARCHITECTS

CLIENTS: UNITED HOUSE DEVELOPMENTS; LONDONEWCASTLE
CONTRACTOR: UNITED HOUSE
PLANNING AUTHORITY: LONDON BOROUGH OF ISLINGTON
IMAGES: POLLARD THOMAS EDWARDS ARCHITECTS

Arundel Square lost one side in the nineteenth century to the
North London railway line. Since then what should have been
a popular Islington address has been blighted. Bill Thomas of
Pollard Thomas Edwards made it his mission to fix it, and after
a sixteen-year battle has helped to deliver 146 apartments in a
block that sits on the railway embankment. The new block comes
with a wonderful new park that includes wild meadow-type
planting on the bund that bridges the railway line. The building
block uses the practice's proven market-pleaser of multiple cores
with two dual-aspect apartments wrapping the lift core and
smaller single-aspect ones in-between. There are penthouses on
top. The eight cores themselves are accessed from the front of
the building through glazed lobbies that enliven comings and
goings. The building is partly faced with Portland stone to reflect
the square's older neighbours, and finished playfully with
coloured-glass balconies.

PEABODY AVENUE
LONDON SW1

HAWORTH TOMPKINS

CLIENT: PEABODY TRUST
CONTRACTOR: MANSELL
PLANNING AUTHORITY: LONDON BOROUGH OF WESTMINSTER
IMAGES: HAWORTH TOMPKINS

Peabody Avenue in London's Pimlico was once one of Peabody's most self-contained estates, a haven alongside the railway lines entering Victoria station. But Victoria's proximity led to bomb damage in the Blitz. Now, some seventy years later, Peabody has restored the missing edge to the estate with fifty-five new apartments and communal facilities in two buildings by Haworth Tompkins. The scheme resembles the original blocks, but the buildings are served by an access gallery to the railway elevation served by cores with lifts at each end. This has allowed Peabody to put wheelchair units on the top level and family ones as duplexes at ground and first-floor level. Upper-level apartments have access to 12- to 14-square-metre balconies cantilevered towards the railway tracks. The scheme plugs into Churchill Gardens' district heating system.

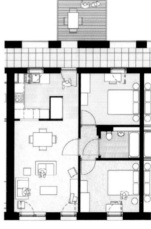

Typical floor plan

ST ANDREWS
LONDON E3

ALLIES AND MORRISON ARCHITECTS; MACCREANOR
LAVINGTON; TOWNSHEND LANDSCAPE ARCHITECTS

CLIENTS: BARRATT LONDON; CIRCLE ANGLIA
CONTRACTOR: BARRATT LONDON
PLANNING AUTHORITY: LONDON BOROUGH OF TOWER HAMLETS
IMAGES: ALLIES AND MORRISON ARCHITECTS; MACCREANOR LAVINGTON

The redevelopment of an NHS site in Bromley-by-Bow led
the developer Barratt London to work closely with the London
Development Agency, the Homes and Communities Agency and
Tower Hamlets Council, the last of which had set a brief for the
site to deliver 30 per cent of the 964 homes planned as family-
sized units. The first two blocks to be completed, one by
Maccreanor Lavington and one by Allies and Morrison, also
the masterplanner, are a modern equivalent of the Edwardian
mansion block, with apartments at up to 130 square metres,
including interlocking duplexes at ground-floor level that have
their own doors to the street. Among the scheme's surprises
are the many and varied outdoor spaces, some screened very
privately within the parapet wall to the roof terraces.

TREES EXTRA CARE HOUSING
LONDON N6

PRP ARCHITECTS

CLIENTS: ONE HOUSING GROUP; HILL HOMES
CONTRACTOR: DURKAN
PLANNING AUTHORITY: LONDON BOROUGH OF HARINGEY
IMAGES: PRP ARCHITECTS

The appointment by Hill Homes of two respected architects to its board to raise procurement quality has led to immediate success. This extra-care scheme is principally three distinct blocks linked by glass bridges that, coupled to a full-height atrium, flood circulation space with daylight. All forty apartments also have glazed balustrades to balconies, another element in a design that works hard to ensure that people who spend more time than average indoors enjoy the benefits of natural light. Detailing of the scheme is especially thorough, reflecting the decision to use a traditional contract that gave PRP control of building, interior design and landscaping. The scheme was jointly developed with One Housing Group, fast becoming a benchmark developer for this category of accommodation, and will be 100 per cent affordable rent in the heart of Highgate, one of London's most exclusive villages.

Typical floor plans

THE AVENUE
SAFFRON WALDEN

POLLARD THOMAS EDWARDS ARCHITECTS

CLIENT: HILL RESIDENTIAL
CONTRACTOR: HILL PARTNERSHIPS
PLANNING AUTHORITY: UTTLESFORD DISTRICT COUNCIL
IMAGES: POLLARD THOMAS EDWARDS ARCHITECTS

The Avenue exploits a tree-lined path across the grounds of
the Friends' School in Saffron Walden, which Ralph Erskine
attended, to create a magical approach to a development of
seventy-six new homes. A row of detached houses is laid out
to one side of the trees, so that cars nip between the trees to
access them. On the opposite side of a new carriageway there
are courtyard clusters that are screened by a continuous brick
wall and accessed through narrow gateways that resemble the
access to a farmyard. The theme continues in the detailing of the
properties, which borrows from the north Essex barn vernacular,
creating a bridge between the bucolic countryside and the
market-town location.

BANK HALL
BRETHERTON, CHORLEY

RICHES HAWLEY MIKHAIL ARCHITECTS

CLIENT: URBAN SPLASH
PLANNING AUTHORITY: CHORLEY BOROUGH COUNCIL
IMAGES: RICHES HAWLEY MIKHAIL ARCHITECTS

Urban Splash has moved out of the city and into the shires with this scheme within the grounds of Bank Hall, a listed building in a remote setting outside the town of Bretherton that has seen a twelve-year campaign to rescue it from crumbling. The latest phase of the campaign to rescue the wreck and its gardens will see twelve apartments and twenty-three houses laid out in two adjacent clusters. There are eight semi-detached 174-square-metre houses to the back of the layout, some pairs connected in an L-shaped plan. Apartments and two- and three-bed houses are contained within terraces of three and four units. The use of a continuous ground-floor brick frontage extended as a boundary treatment picks up on a walled garden within the hall's grounds.

Section

BOLD AS BRICK
PRESTON

RCKA

CLIENT: COMMUNITY GATEWAY ASSOCIATION
PLANNING AUTHORITY: PRESTON CITY COUNCIL
IMAGES: RCKA

Key to the competition brief was the need to redevelop this shallow site with homes that surveilled the streets around them. The southernmost street has no vehicular access, so its mostly two-storey three-bed houses have their cars parked in the gaps between the three-storey four-bed properties on the northern perimeter, which overlook a home zone where their cars are parked. Gardens interlock in a saw-tooth arrangement, and properties on the southernmost street can be accessed either from the street or through the garden to their rear. The three-storey houses have a further room at first-floor level that can be used as a dining room. The scheme reinvents the brick façade familiar to this part of Lancashire.

CAMBRIDGE & WELLS COURT
LONDON NW6

LIFSCHUTZ DAVIDSON SANDILANDS

CLIENT/PLANNING AUTHORITY: LONDON BOROUGH OF BRENT
IMAGES: LIFSCHUTZ DAVIDSON SANDILANDS

There hasn't been much council housing since the 1970s, so this
scheme by London Borough of Brent has the potential to be the
best in forty years. It is part of an area-wide regeneration of south
Kilburn that replaces post-war slab blocks in open space with
a distinctly familiar London street pattern and building form.
Disguised within the four-storey terraced houses that mirror the
semi-detached villas opposite them are dual-aspect apartments
with private outdoor spaces to the rear, accessed by cores that
link the new villas. Behind is another recognisably London form,
a mews that puts family-sized duplexes on the top floors
complete with large secure outdoor space on the terrace. The
design by Lifschutz Davidson Sandilands even uses a traditional
London brick for robust detailing.

NEW ISLINGTON – THE GUTS
MANCHESTER

MAE LLP ARCHITECTS

CLIENT: GREAT PLACES HOUSING GROUP
CONTRACTOR: MANSELL
PLANNING AUTHORITY: MANCHESTER CITY COUNCIL
IMAGES: MAE LLP ARCHITECTS

The masterplan for New Islington in Manchester has several
strips of land left from the demolished Cardroom estate that are
too shallow to lay out houses to each street and enclose gardens
behind. One parcel of this design is a variation on courtyard
houses, turning semi-detached units sideways so that the party
wall is now the boundary between two properties, one facing
north and the other south. It then puts private outdoor space
between each pair of houses, thus creating both secure off-street
parking (a key part of the brief) and a small private garden and
first-floor terrace that are overlooked only by the house to which
they belong. The boundary to the front of each house is
protected by a low brick wall and has a deep recessed porch.

PORTOBELLO SQUARE
LONDON W10

PRP ARCHITECTS

CLIENT: CATALYST HOUSING GROUP
CONTRACTOR: MANSELL
PLANNING AUTHORITY: THE ROYAL BOROUGH OF KENSINGTON AND
    CHELSEA
IMAGES: PRP ARCHITECTS

This first phase of the redevelopment of the troubled Wornington Green estate in London's North Kensington will see 324 new homes built on a street pattern that replicates the Victorian streets before their flawed post-war redevelopment. New buildings take their cues from the capital's older typologies, with terraces of grand town houses and mews, as well as apartments overlooking a new square in the manner of the mansion blocks that line London's parks. The area's high property values mean that most of the four-storey town houses will be for market sale, making these streets a rare offering among the capital's extensive redevelopment. Building details will also pick up on the Georgian tradition of brick and stonework, updated with crisp fenestration.

ST BEDES
BEDFORD

PRP ARCHITECTS

CLIENT: ORBIT HOMES
PLANNING AUTHORITY: BEDFORD BOROUGH COUNCIL
IMAGES: PRP ARCHITECTS

PRP Architects was represented on the expert panel behind the 2009 governmental report *Housing our Ageing Population: Panel for Innovation* (HAPPI). Some of the recommendations are reflected in this design for the redevelopment of a school site, which will put a new extra-care development of 104 apartments close to key amenities in Bedford. One elevation to the scheme mimics the villas in the surrounding street, and connects the units with glass bridges so that residents experience the street as they circulate within the apartment block. Deck accesses line the secure courtyard garden, helping to ensure that residents receive regular doses of daylight as they move about, while generous balconies to the street elevations offer the same benefit.

PREVIOUS WINNERS AND ROYAL GOLD MEDALLISTS

THE RIBA STIRLING PRIZE

1996 Hodder Associates, University of Salford

1997 Michael Wilford and Partners, Music School, Stuttgart

1998 Foster + Partners, American Air Museum, Duxford

1999 Future Systems, NatWest Media Centre, Lord's, London

2000 Alsop & Störmer, Peckham Library and Media Centre, London

2001 Wilkinson Eyre Architects, Magna, Rotherham

2002 Wilkinson Eyre Architects, Millennium Bridge, Gateshead

2003 Herzog & de Meuron, Laban, London

2004 Foster + Partners, 30 St Mary Axe, London

2005 EMBT/RMJM, The Scottish Parliament, Edinburgh

2006 Richard Rogers Partnership with Estudio Lamela, New Area Terminal, Barajas Airport, Madrid

2007 David Chipperfield Architects, Museum of Modern Literature, Marbach am Neckar

2008 Feilden Clegg Bradley Studios, Alison Brooks Architects, Maccreanor Lavington, Accordia, Cambridge

2009 Rogers Stirk Harbour + Partners, Maggie's London

2010 Zaha Hadid Architects, MAXXI, Museo Nazionale delle Arti del XXI Secolo, Rome

THE RIBA LUBETKIN PRIZE

2006 Noero Wolff Architects, Red Location Museum of the People's Struggle, New Brighton, South Africa

2007 Grimshaw (Grimshaw Jackson Joint Venture), Southern Cross Station, Melbourne, Australia

2008 Gianni Botsford Architects, Casa Kike, Cahuita, Costa Rica

2009 Herzog & de Meuron, The National Stadium, Beijing

2010 Heatherwick Studio, UK Pavilion, Expo 2010 Shanghai, China

THE RIBA MANSER MEDAL

2001 Cezary Bednarski, Merthyr Terrace, London

2002 Burd Haward Marston Architects, Brooke Coombes House, London

2003 Jamie Fobert Architects, Anderson House, London

2004 Mole Architects, Black House, Cambridgeshire

2005 Robert Dye Associates, Stealth House, London

2006 Knox Bhavan Architects, Holly Barn, Norfolk

2007 Alison Brooks Architects, The Salt House, St Lawrence Bay

2008 Rogers Stirk Harbour + Partners, Oxley Woods, Milton Keynes

2009 Pitman Tozer Architects, Gap House, London

2010 Acme, Hunsett Mill, Stalham, Norfolk

THE STEPHEN LAWRENCE PRIZE

1998 Ian Ritchie Architects, Terrasson Cultural Greenhouse, France

1999 Munkenbeck + Marshall, Sculpture Gallery, Roche Court, near Salisbury

2000 Softroom Architects, Kielder Belvedere, Northumberland

2001 Richard Rose-Casemore, Hatherley Studio, Winchester

2002 Cottrell + Vermeulen Architecture, Cardboard Building, Westborough Primary School, Westcliff-on-Sea

2003 Gumuchdjian Architects, Think Tank, Skibbereen

2004 Simon Conder Associates, Vista, Dungeness

2005 Níall McLaughlin Architects, House at Clonakilty, County Cork

2006 Alison Brooks Architects, Wrap House, London

2007 David Sheppard Architects, Wooda, Crackington Haven

2008 John Pawson, The Sackler Crossing, Royal Botanic Gardens, Kew, Richmond

2009 Simon Conder Associates, El Ray, Dungeness

2010 Gumuchdjian Architects, Artists' House, London

THE RIBA CLIENT OF THE YEAR

1998 Roland Paoletti: new Jubilee line stations, London

1999 MCC: buildings at Lord's Cricket Ground, London

2000 Foreign & Commonwealth Office: embassies around the world

2001 Molendinar Park Housing Association, Glasgow: buildings by various Scottish architects

2002 Urban Splash: regeneration in Manchester and Liverpool

2003 City of Manchester: post-IRA-bomb projects

2004 Peabody Trust: RIBA Award-winning schemes

2005 Gateshead Council: art and architecture projects

2006 Royal Botanic Gardens: buildings at Kew and Wakehurst Place

2007 Derwent London: 28 Dorset Square, London

2008 Coin Street Community Builders: Coin Street Neighbourhood Centre, London

2009 Camden & Islington Community Solutions: Kentish Town Health Centre, London; Grosvenor: Liverpool One Masterplan; Kielder Partnership: Kielder Observatory, Northumberland; Maggie's: Maggie's London; Parabola Land: Kings Place, London; St Martin-in-the-Fields, London

2010 Hammerson: 60 Threadneedle Street, London; Twenty Bishops Square/St Botolph's Hall, London

THE ARCHITECTS' JOURNAL FIRST BUILDING AWARD

2001 Walker Architecture, Cedar House, Logiealmond, Scotland

2002 Sutherland Hussey Architects, Barnhouse, London

2003 dRMM, No. 1 Centaur Street, London

2004 Annalie Riches, Silvia Ullmayer and Barti Garibaldo, In Between, London

2005 Amin Taha Architects, Gazzano House, London

THE CROWN ESTATE CONSERVATION AWARD

1998 Peter Inskip + Peter Jenkins, Temple of Concord and Victory, Stowe

1999 Foster + Partners, Reichstag, Berlin

2000 Foster + Partners, JC Decaux UK Headquarters, Brentford

2001 Rick Mather Architects, Dulwich Picture Gallery, London

2002 Richard Murphy Architects with Simpson Brown Architects, Stirling Tolbooth, Scotland

2003 LDN Architects, Newhailes House, Musselburgh, Scotland

2004 HOK International, King's Library at the British Museum, London

2005 Avanti Architects, Isokon (Lawn Road) Apartments, London

2006 Dixon Jones with Purcell Miller Tritton, the National Gallery East Wing and Central Portico, London

2007 Alec French Architects, SS *Great Britain* and Historic Dockyard, Bristol

2008 Alastair Lansley (for Union Railways), St Pancras International, London

2009 Union North, The Midland Hotel, Morecambe

2010 David Chipperfield Architects in collaboration with Julian Harrap, Neues Museum, Museuminsel, Berlin

THE ADAPT TRUST ACCESS AWARD

2001 Avery Associates Architects, Royal Academy of Dramatic Arts, London

2002 Malcolm Fraser Architects, Dance Base, Edinburgh

2003 Nicoll Russell Studios, The Space, Dundee College

THE RIBA INCLUSIVE DESIGN AWARD

2004   Arup Associates, City of Manchester Stadium

2005   Foster + Partners, Sage, Gateshead

2006   Adjaye/Associates, Idea Store, Whitechapel, London

2007   Patel Taylor, Portland College New Learning Centre,
Mansfield

THE RIBA CABE PUBLIC SPACE AWARD

2008   Gustafson Porter, Old Market Square,
Nottingham

2009   McDowell + Benedetti Architects, Castleford Bridge,
Castleford

2010   AECOM Design + Planning, Pier Head and Canal Link,
Georges Parade, Liverpool

THE RIBA SUSTAINABILITY AWARD

2000   Chetwood Associates, Sainsbury's, Greenwich, London

2001   Michael Hopkins and Partners, Jubilee Campus, University
of Nottingham

2002   Cottrell + Vermeulen Architecture, Cardboard Building,
Westborough Primary School, Westcliff-on-Sea

2003   Bill Dunster Architects, BedZED, Wallington

2004   Sarah Wigglesworth Architects, Stock Orchard Street,
London

2005   Associated Architects, Cobtun House, Worcester

2006   Feilden Clegg Bradley Architects, Heelis, Swindon

2007   Architype, Upper Twyford Barns, Hereford

2008   Denton Corker Marshall, Manchester Civil Justice Centre

THE RIBA SORRELL FOUNDATION SCHOOLS AWARD

2007   Building Design Partnership, Marlowe Academy,
Ramsgate

2008   Allford Hall Monaghan Morris, Westminster Academy at
the Naim Dangoor Centre, London

2009   Penoyre & Prasad, The Minster School, Southwell

2010   Architype, St Luke's Church of England Aided Primary
School, Wolverhampton

ROYAL GOLD MEDALLISTS

The Royal Gold Medal for the promotion of architecture, instituted
by Queen Victoria in 1848, is conferred annually by the sovereign
on some distinguished architect or group of architects for work of
high merit, or on some distinguished person or group whose work
has promoted either directly or indirectly the advancement of
architecture.

1848   Charles Robert Cockerell, RA

1849   Luigi Canina, Italy

1850   Sir Charles Barry, RA

1851   Thomas L. Donaldson

1852   Leo von Klenze, Austria

1853   Sir Robert Smirke, RA

1854   Philip Hardwick, RA

1855   J.I. Hittorff, France

1856   Sir William Tite

1857   Owen Jones

1858   August Stuler, Germany

1859   Sir George Gilbert Scott, RA

1860   Sydney Smirke, RA

1861   J.B. Lesueur, France

1862   Revd Robert Willis

1863   Anthony Salvin

1864   E. Viollet-le-Duc, France

1865   Sir James Pennethorne

1866   Sir M. Digby Wyatt

1867   Charles Texier, France

1868   Sir Henry Layard

1869   C.R. Lepsius, Germany

1870   Benjamin Ferrey

1871   James Fergusson

1872   Baron von Schmidt, Austria

1873   Thomas Henry Wyatt

1874   George Edmund Street, RA

1875   Edmund Sharpe

1876   Joseph Louis Duc, France

1877   Charles Barry

1878   Alfred Waterhouse, RA

1879   Marquis de Vogue, France

1880   John L. Pearson, RA

1881   George Godwin

1882   Baron von Ferstel, Austria

1883	Francis Cranmer Penrose	1922	Thomas Hastings, USA
1884	William Butterfield	1923	Sir John James Burnet, FRIAS, RA, RSA
1885	H. Schliemann, Germany	1924	Not awarded
1886	Charles Garnier, France	1925	Sir Giles Gilbert Scott, OM, DCL, RA
1887	Ewan Christian	1926	Professor Ragnar Östberg, Sweden
1888	Baron von Hansen, Austria	1927	Sir Herbert Baker, KCIE, RA
1889	Sir Charles T. Newton	1928	Sir Guy Dawber, RA, FSA
1890	John Gibson	1929	Victor Alexandre Frederic Laloux, France
1891	Sir Arthur Blomfield, ARA	1930	Percy Scott Worthington, FSA
1892	César Daly, France	1931	Sir Edwin Cooper, RA
1893	Richard Morris Hunt, USA	1932	Dr Hendrik Petrus Berlage, The Netherlands
1894	Lord Leighton, RA	1933	Sir Charles Reed Peers, CBE, PPSA
1895	James Brooks	1934	Henry Vaughan Lanchester, PPTPI
1896	Sir Ernest George, RA	1935	Willem Marinus Dudok, The Netherlands
1897	Dr P.J.H. Cuypers, The Netherlands	1936	Charles Henry Holden, MTPI
1898	George Aitchison, RA	1937	Sir Raymond Unwin
1899	George Frederick Bodley, RA	1938	Professor Ivar Tengbom, Sweden
1900	Professor Rodolfo Amadeo Lanciani, Italy	1939	Sir Percy Thomas, OBE, JP, MTPI
1901	Not awarded, owing to the death of Queen Victoria	1940	Charles Francis Annesley Voysey
1902	Thomas Edward Collcutt	1941	Frank Lloyd Wright, USA
1903	Charles F. McKim, USA	1942	William Curtis Green, RA
1904	Auguste Choisy, France	1943	Professor Sir Charles Herbert Reilly, OBE
1905	Sir Aston Webb, PPRA	1944	Sir Edward Maufe, RA
1906	Sir L. Alma-Tadema, RA	1945	Victor Vessnin, USSR
1907	John Belcher, RA	1946	Professor Sir Patrick Abercrombie, FSA, PPTPI, FILA
1908	Honoré Daumet, France	1947	Professor Sir Albert Edward Richardson, RA, FSA
1909	Sir Arthur John Evans, FRS, FSA	1948	Auguste Perret, France
1910	Sir Thomas Graham Jackson	1949	Sir Howard Robertson, MC, ARA, SADG
1911	Wilhelm Dorpfeld, Germany	1950	Eliel Saarinen, USA
1912	Basil Champneys	1951	Emanuel Vincent Harris, OBE, RA
1913	Sir Reginald Blomfield, RA, FSA	1952	George Grey Wornum
1914	Jean Louis Pascal, France	1953	Le Corbusier (C.E. Jeanneret), France
1915	Frank Darling, Canada	1954	Sir Arthur George Stephenson, CMG, AMTPI, Australia
1916	Sir Robert Rowand Anderson, FRIAS	1955	John Murray Easton
1917	Henri Paul Nenot, Membre de l'Institut, France	1956	Dr Walter Adolf Georg Gropius, USA
1918	Ernest Newton, RA	1957	Hugo Alvar Henrik Aalto, Finland
1919	Leonard Stokes	1958	Robert Schofield Morris, FRAIC, Canada
1920	Charles Louis Girault, Membre de l'Institut, France	1959	Professor Ludwig Mies van der Rohe, USA
1921	Sir Edwin Landseer Lutyens, OM, KCIE, RA, FSA	1960	Professor Pier Luigi Nervi, Italy

1961	Lewis Mumford, USA		**1999**	The City of Barcelona, Spain
1962	Professor Sven Gottfried Markelius, Sweden		**2000**	Frank Gehry, USA
1963	Lord Holford, ARA, PPTPI, FILA		**2001**	Jean Nouvel, France
1964	E. Maxwell Fry, CBE		**2002**	Archigram
1965	Professor Kenzo Tange, Japan		**2003**	Rafael Moneo, Spain
1966	Ove Arup, CBE, MICE, MIStructE		**2004**	Rem Koolhaas, The Netherlands
1967	Sir Nikolaus Pevsner, CBE, FBA, FSA, Hon ARIBA		**2005**	Frei Otto, Germany
1968	Dr Richard Buckminster Fuller, FRSA, Hon AIA, USA		**2006**	Toyo Ito, Japan
			2007	Jacques Herzog and Pierre de Meuron, Switzerland
1969	Jack Antonio Coia, CBE, RSA, AMTPI, FRIAS		**2008**	Edward Cullinan, CBE
1970	Professor Sir Robert Matthew, CBE, ARSA, FRIAS		**2009**	Álvaro Siza, Portugal
			2010	I.M. Pei, USA

1961 Lewis Mumford, USA

1962 Professor Sven Gottfried Markelius, Sweden

1963 Lord Holford, ARA, PPTPI, FILA

1964 E. Maxwell Fry, CBE

1965 Professor Kenzo Tange, Japan

1966 Ove Arup, CBE, MICE, MIStructE

1967 Sir Nikolaus Pevsner, CBE, FBA, FSA, Hon ARIBA

1968 Dr Richard Buckminster Fuller, FRSA, Hon AIA, USA

1969 Jack Antonio Coia, CBE, RSA, AMTPI, FRIAS

1970 Professor Sir Robert Matthew, CBE, ARSA, FRIAS

1971 Hubert de Cronin Hastings

1972 Louis I. Kahn, USA

1973 Sir Leslie Martin

1974 Powell & Moya

1975 Michael Scott, Ireland

1976 Sir John Summerson, CBE, FBA, FSA

1977 Sir Denys Lasdun, CBE

1978 Jørn Utzon, Denmark

1979 The Office of Charles and Ray Eames, USA

1980 James Stirling

1981 Sir Philip Dowson, CBE

1982 Berthold Lubetkin

1983 Sir Norman Foster

1984 Charles Correa, India

1985 Sir Richard Rogers

1986 Arata Isozaki, Japan

1987 Ralph Erskine, CBE

1988 Richard Meier, USA

1989 Renzo Piano, Italy

1990 Aldo van Eyck, The Netherlands

1991 Colin Stansfield Smith, CBE

1992 Peter Rice, DIC(IC), MICE

1993 Giancarlo de Carlo, Italy

1994 Michael and Patricia Hopkins

1995 Colin Rowe, USA

1996 Harry Seidler, Australia

1997 Tadao Ando, Japan

1998 Oscar Niemeyer, Brazil

1999 The City of Barcelona, Spain

2000 Frank Gehry, USA

2001 Jean Nouvel, France

2002 Archigram

2003 Rafael Moneo, Spain

2004 Rem Koolhaas, The Netherlands

2005 Frei Otto, Germany

2006 Toyo Ito, Japan

2007 Jacques Herzog and Pierre de Meuron, Switzerland

2008 Edward Cullinan, CBE

2009 Álvaro Siza, Portugal

2010 I.M. Pei, USA

This list includes honorific titles at the time of the award and professional but not academic qualifications.

SPONSORS AND SUPPORTERS

The RIBA is extremely grateful to all the sponsors and supporters who make the awards possible.

Every week since 1895 *The Architects' Journal* has celebrated the achievements of British architects in its pages. Known to architects as the *AJ*, the magazine believes that the architectural profession benefits from having a single pre-eminent and undisputed award for quality design. That is why it has supported the RIBA Stirling Prize for more than a decade, helping it to become recognized as marking the highest achievement in UK architecture by both the profession and the general public.

This year Kingspan Benchmark launched Kingspan Benchmark Connect, a pre-engineered multi-spanning unitized wall system that has excellent thermal, structural and fire performance and can speed up the build time while providing the ideal platform for the Benchmark façade range. Also recently launched is Benchmark Evolution, the latest development in insulated panel technology. Evolution is a stylish, sleek laser flat panel with a unique range of design features that allow maximum flexibility in the creation of a truly bespoke system.

HSBC Private Bank is proud to partner with the RIBA as exclusive sponsor of the RIBA Manser Medal. This partnership builds on the bank's long-established commitment to design while underlining its respect for clients, architects and other professionals who create inspiring houses through exceptional design. HSBC Private Bank and the RIBA are leaders in their respective fields with a shared commitment to excellence. HSBC Private Bank has unrivalled property-lending expertise for private clients in the UK, as well as providing expert advice for clients seeking outstanding homes.

The Marco Goldschmied Foundation continues its fourteen-year-long support for the Stephen Lawrence Prize, established in memory of the murdered teenager who aspired to be an architect. The Foundation provides the £5000 prize money and funds a £10,000 Stephen Lawrence Scholarship at the Architectural Association in London.

The Bloxham Charitable Trust

The first RIBA Client of the Year was named in 1998. The award recognizes the role that good clients play in the delivery of fine architecture. The fifth winner, in 2002, was Urban Splash, for 'its commitment both to design and quality and the regeneration of Manchester and Liverpool'. Urban Splash's co-founder Tom Bloxham now supports the award through the Bloxham Charitable Trust.

RIBA Award plaques are produced and donated by the Lead Sheet Association (LSA). The LSA is the primary independent body involved in the promotion and development of the use of rolled-lead sheet. The LSA is proud to have been associated with the RIBA Awards since 1989.

IBSTOCK ®
building sustainability

Ibstock and the RIBA have a long history of working together. This fruitful relationship has helped to maintain the close affinity that architects have with the use of brick and clay products as a natural and sustainable cladding material. Ibstock is proud to continue to support and sponsor the work and aims of the RIBA.

With more than thirty-five years' experience, NBS understands the importance of producing top-class specifications. Consequently, the UK construction industry turns to NBS for a master specification system producing technically robust, up-to-date project specifications. Continuing its customer commitment, NBS is entering an exciting phase with a new concept in specification, NBS Create. NBS Create allows customers the flexibility to write different types of specifications, to extend the use of specifications throughout the life of a project, and to enable better collaboration, whether with clients, contractors or anyone involved in the process.

INDEX

TONY CHAPMAN is Head of Awards at the Royal Institute of British Architects. He has been, in vaguely chronological order, a bookseller, librarian, actor, playwright, theatre director, TV researcher/director/producer and architectural bureaucrat. While at the BBC he made a number of programmes about architecture and planning, including the modernists' riposte to Prince Charles's *A Vision of Britain* with then RIBA President Maxwell Hutchinson. He was thus considered by the RIBA to be a safe pair of hands to run its press office and latterly its awards programme, which includes, as well as the RIBA Awards and Stirling Prize, the RIBA Lubetkin Prize, the European Contemporary Architecture Prize and the Royal Gold Medal. He was made an Honorary Fellow of the RIBA in 2011.

The RIBA should like to thank all the awards judges, who give freely of their time and whose reports form the basis of much of the text of this book.

The RIBA also thanks the photographers whose work is published in this book and who agreed to waive copyright fees for the reproduction of their work in connection with the RIBA's promotion of the awards.

Photography/illustration credits are provided on page for all award-winning projects. Other images in this book have been reproduced courtesy of the following copyright holders:

Mohammad Akram: 205; Sue Barr – VIEW: 91, 99; Joakim Boren: 89; Michael Boyd: 198 bottom; James Brittain – VIEW: 96; Tim Brotherton: 92 top; Richard Bryant – Arcaid: 197, 203 top; Peter Cook – VIEW: 95; Tim Crocker: 90; David Chipperfield Architects: 198 centre; Glenn Dearing: 190; Lyndon Douglas: 82; Featherstone Young: 84, 92 bottom; Rob 't Hart: 208; Andrew Lee: 93; Living Architecture: 81; Mississauga Images: 207; James Morris – VIEW: 85; Olympic Delivery Authority: 9; Jens Passoth: 209; Paul Raftery – VIEW: 206; Adam Richards: 83; Christian Richters – VIEW: 10 top, 198 top, 201, 203 bottom; Paul Riddle – VIEW: 97; Timothy Soar: 10 bottom; Paul Tyagi: 98